The U.S. Economy Demystified

The U.S. Economy Demystified

What the Major Economic Statistics Mean and Their Significance for Business

Revised Edition

Albert T. Sommers
The Conference Board

with Lucie R. Blau

Lexington Books
D.C. Heath and Company/Lexington, Massachusetts/Toronto

Sommers, Albert T.
The U.S. economy demystified : what the major economic statistics
mean and their significance for business / Albert T. Sommers (The
Conference Board) with Lucie R. Blau.
    p.   cm.
    Includes index.
    ISBN 0–669–17383–5 (alk. paper).
    ISBN 0–669–17385–1 (pbk. : alk. paper)
    1.   United States—Economic conditions—1945–   2.   United States—
Economic policy.   3.   National income—United States—Accounting.
I.   Blau, Lucie R.   II.   Conference Board.   III.   Title.   IV.   Title:
United States economy demystified.
HC106.5.S64   1988
330.973'0927–dc19   87–27587

Published simultaneously in Canada
Printed in the United States of America
Casebound International Standard Book Number: 0–669–17383–5
Paperbound International Standard Book Number: 0–669–17385–1
Library of Congress Catalog Card Number 84–48451

The paper used in this publication meets the minimum requirements of
American National Standard for Information Sciences—Permanence of
Paper for Printed Library Materials, ANSI Z39.48–1984. ∞™

88 89 90 91 92 8 7 6 5 4 3 2

Contents

Figures

Tables

Foreword

This book developed out of the author's experience over three decades in explaining the workings of the U.S. economic system and the significance of economic statistics to the thousands of business executives and government officials, here and abroad, who constitute The Conference Board audience. The statistical materials with which it deals, and the economic and philosophical questions to which it addresses itself, are drawn out of long exposure to the interests expressed by intelligent laypersons on how this immensely fascinating economic system works, and how the evidence of its workings can be observed. Mr. Sommers writes as he speaks—lucidly, and with ingratiating humility regarding the uncertainties of data, and the limits of economic reasoning.

Lucie R. Blau, the author's long-time research associate, worked prodigiously on the underlying statistics, contributed to the design of the figures and tables, and supervised the preparation of the text for publication. Virgil Koch, of The Conference Board's graphic department, was in charge of the artwork, under the supervision of Chuck N. Tow, The Conference Board's chief chartist. Beatrice Beirne managed the text through its several drafts, on her beloved word processor. The book is really a joint product of all these people.

James T. Mills, President
The Conference Board

Preface to the Second Edition

Since the first edition of this book went to press two years ago, the U.S. economy has behaved in mysterious ways that have confounded the efforts of governmental and private economists to forecast its near-term course or even to understand its behavior in the recent past. To state the dilemma simply, in the years since 1984, domestic economic conditions have remained seriously sluggish and on the whole unsatisfactory in the face of massive stimuli provided by economic policy itself, as well as by such presumably favorable accidents as an enormous reduction in the price of crude oil and petroleum products. This apparent paradox—the unseemly reluctance of the system to enjoy circumstances that virtually all forecasters considered highly favorable—does not reflect defects in the statistical system itself, and the chapters of this book concerned primarily with such matters have required very little revision. But other chapters that deal more substantively with the behavior of the system—particularly, the behavior of the financial side of the system—have required some rewriting, and here and there considerable amplification. Finally, pursuit of an explanation of the paradox has called for additional material on the historical development of the United States over several decades and the bearing of that history on its recent and prospective economic behavior. If there was a serious omission in the portrait of the U.S. economy provided by the first edition, it was the absence of an interpretive view of the history that has brought it to where it is today.

In these new materials, and in the additions and revisions of later chapters in the book, a sense of urgency appears—an impression that large and unfamiliar issues confront the U.S. economy, and therefore its business leaders, its government policymakers, and inevitably its citizens both as producers and as consumers. Dealing with emerging and still evolving issues in which evidence and perception can change rapidly is awkward material for a book, with its inevitably lengthy production schedule. This poses a risk for reader and writer alike—the risk of high perishability. But there is no way of avoiding the risk at this critical juncture in the course of the U.S. economy.

Accordingly, the first chapter of this new edition is devoted to a longer-term view of the U.S. economic condition, tracing the roots of the present back more than a half-century to the Great Depression. Many of the crucial threads of this history — the altered structure of inflation, the changing nature of the financial market, the violent involution of the U.S. position in the world — are enlarged upon in the appropriate ensuing chapters.

As the publisher, using impeccable economic analysis, has observed, the appearance of a second edition is dependent on the success of the first. I am indeed pleased by the reception accorded the first edition. Individuals in business and government have apparently found it to be a helpful guide. Equally gratifying has been the extensive use of the paperbound version as a supplement in various undergraduate economics courses. Demand here has far exceeded my expectations — and the publisher's — another example of the difficulties inherent in forecasting economic behavior.

Introduction

Immensely powerful, ever changing, pulsating with a hundred different rhythms, and offering every conceivable combination of economic risk and reward, the U.S. economy ranks as one of the wonders of the world. As a subject for detached intellectual study, it offers fascinations and degrees of complexity unsurpassed by any structures in the physical world.

But it is, of course, more than that: It is the natural habitat in which we live, work, save, spend, plan, invest. Each of us can expect to grow familiar with, and then finally expert in, the area of this structure in which we make our own careers; but each area is inseparably bound to the whole, and often takes its course from conditions and trends arising in distant parts of the system. The prosperity of families, businesses, and even governmental units in the structure depends not only on sophisticated adjustment to the local environment, but also on a reasonable grasp of the course of the whole system. That, in turn, requires some facility in reading and interpreting the awesome profusion of signals thrown off by the economic system as it makes its way through time. The collection and processing of these signals is an industry in itself, largely but not exclusively in the hands of government agencies.

If the U.S. economy is a wonder to behold, this book is about how to behold it. It is not for professional economists, who spend their lives creating, handling, and interpreting the kinds of information offered here. Instead, it is for the sophisticated businessman, the financial executive, the private investor, even the alert individual consumer, who seek a compact, digestible guide to the general evidence on economic conditions, and require a framework within which to insert new information as it appears in the media — who want to apply their own practical intelligence to the question of where the U.S. economy is, judging from its statistical condition, and where it is likely to go. It will not make the reader his own economist (there are those who say there are too many around already); but a reasonably careful study should considerably improve his ability to understand the evidence, to keep track of it, to develop confidence in his knowledge of current economic events, and to sense the probable range of future developments.

The first chapter of this book puts the present position of the U.S. economy in a long historical perspective that is essential to understanding its present behavior and the issues it confronts in the remainder of this decade. The next two chapters lay out the essentials of the U.S. statistical system, starting with the national accounting system, without which no understanding of the position and course of the economy is really possible, and moving on to brief descriptions of the basic array of statistics that describe U.S. economic performance. Chapter 4 explains the nature of the business cycle and the statistics by which this powerful tidal current in the system can be observed and measured. Chapter 5 deals with the influences exerted on the course of the system by the conscious decisions of government with respect to the course of the federal budget, the availability and price of credit, and the general (recently spectacular) behavior of the financial markets. Chapter 6 places the U.S. economy in its world context; it treats briefly those statistical relationships that describe our place in the world economy and the consequences that flow from our international behavior. Chapter 7 interprets the evidence on U.S. performance with respect to inflation—the enemy that awaits the system when it loses its coherence or when it seeks excessively costly goals.

Much of standard economics treats economic life as transpiring in a so-called free market, in which individual self-interest rules supreme. This is not the way the real world works, of course; some of the greatest difficulties in understanding the behavior of the economy reflect this disparity between theory and reality. Accordingly, a final chapter, more reflective and less numerical, appraises the U.S. economy as a component of a total sociological structure subject to social, political, and ethical pressures that often influence its course and limit its options.

1
The Long Wave of History

Any effort to comprehend, and then to explain, an economic system must begin not with theory, and not with statistics, but with history. At all times, and for all nations, economic systems are the product of an evolutionary process; they carry their history with them—if not visibly on their surfaces, then deep inside, in mechanisms and structures that affect their course in the future. The events of the past few weeks or even the past few years color and shape the present and shed light on where the system will go next. But even far more distant events—rhythms born even decades ago—may still be pulsing in the system, influencing its behavior in ways that are unpredictable from the evidence at the surface. Great wars, great depressions, great booms are not passing events whose significance disappears as the events themselves come to an end; they are capable of reorganizing and redirecting economic systems, throwing them into new trajectories that can run for decades, producing economic experience that cannot be understood without reference to them.

If this is true of all economies at all times, it is spectacularly true of the U.S. economy today. The record of its particular past, traceable back to great events a half-century ago, is controlling much of its behavior, producing results—in the real economy, and in the behavior of its financial sector—that are inexplicable without reference to its history. Here, in these understudied and partly forgotten roots of the future, is where we must begin.

Any observer of the American economic scene over several decades would almost certainly agree with the observation that life in the U.S. economy is now more complex, more difficult to understand, and more hazardous to predict than it used to be. In particular, the two conventional modalities of economic forecasting—the eighteen-month, short-term forecast, and the ten-year, long-term projection—carry very little of the conviction they seemed to convey to businesspersons and policymakers even a decade ago. The tools of short-term economic analysis have grown so dull and unenlightening that they have been partially abandoned for the past several years. The typical short-term economic forecast running quarterly for eighteen months or so into the future has been unrewarding in the extreme. It is commonly observed that the business cycle, on which such short-term forecasting depended, has apparently atrophied. (Not so; see chapter 4.)

The decade-long projections also seem to have fallen into disuse. To project ten years out takes a long base of past data, on a kind of cantilever principle; but it is hard to find long economic series that seem to retain relevance for the radically different domestic and international circumstances in which the United States has found itself in the 1980s. Long-term projections, drawn out of long-term calculations of past trends, almost necessarily take a linear form. The turbulent, volatile history of the U.S. economy over the past decade hardly seems to be effectively expressed by linear projection.

In this decade, economics has thus seemed to provide little real guidance either to economic policy or to the management of real and financial assets. This is not a matter of inadequate information or failures of economic reasoning; the data and intellectual resources available to economists, as they are reviewed in later chapters of this book, are impressive, and they worked well for decades. But more than ever before, they seem to require a coherent, historically based view of how the system got here, and therefore a view of the forces carrying it into the future. A description of the current U.S. economic position as reflecting history, even a "long wave" of history—a complex, nonlinear trajectory, incorporating in its later phases the fortunes of many of our trading partners—seems to offer a perspective essential to our purposes here. It seems to clarify the present and illuminate the main issues of the future. It heightens the sense of danger that is now felt, and more and more expressed, by economists and financial analysts; but it also provides some essential understanding of what the dangers are, and what requirements they impose on us, if they are to be averted.

Historical Origins; the Big Bang

Where to start such a history? For once, economics provides an unequivocal answer. Conditions prevailing at the end of World War II—almost exactly forty years ago—qualify spectacularly as a time of gross discordance in world economic conditions, containing a huge (without question the biggest in history) volume of static economic energy available to the United States—an unprecedented voltage accumulated over ten years of worldwide depression and then five years of very nearly total war. This massive disruption of the normal course of history—the gross and prolonged deferrals of the ordinary satisfactions of life—marks the beginning of modern history.

In the years of the Great Depression, the American economic system was reshaped and its history restarted. The structure of private debt was collapsed

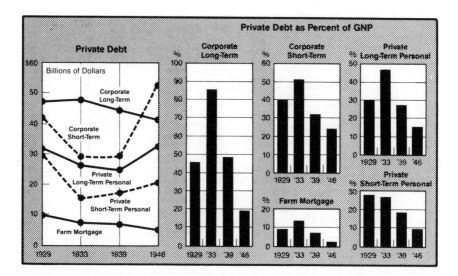

Sources: U.S. Department of Commerce; The Conference Board.

Figure 1–1. Fifteen Years of Low Debt Formation

by bankruptcy, repossession, and default, in an environment that tolerated little or no new debt incurrence. (See figure 1–1.) At the same time, levels of holdings of real assets shriveled in the virtual absence of new production. The shrunken stock of physical assets that survived the Depression was old in years, and old relative to the technology available at the end of the Depression (technological development, but not commercialization of the findings, continued at a rapid rate even under depression conditions). At the end of the thirties, the U.S. system was depleted, even near exhaustion, in all its physical dimensions; it carried large deficits in the physical stock of goods required to maintain predepression living standards. (See figure 1–2.)

The ensuing five years of total war continued to suppress the level of real nondefense assets, whose average technological age continued to lengthen. But whole new ranges of technology, developed initially for military purposes but holding vast promise for commercial exploitation, accumulated during the war. The war also produced another crucial requirement for explosive growth that only war is likely to generate: an enormous increase in liquidity, reflecting the gigantic financial requirements of a wartime government and the absolute necessity for the central bank to provide the financing. The financing of the war produced a "Keynesian shock" of liquidity growth—an outpouring of cash as a counterpart of federally financed deficits—that was a vast multiple of anything that Keynes himself envisioned as a cure for the

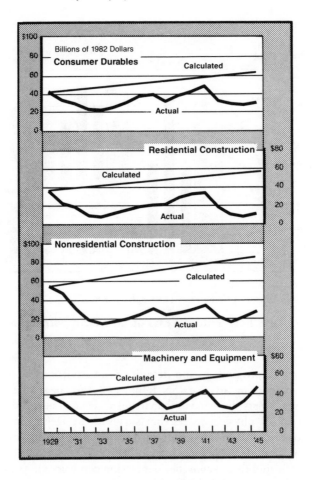

Note: Deficits between actual and calculated demands, 1929–1945; calculated series represent cumulative growth from 1929, at 3 percent per annum.

Sources: U.S. Department of Commerce; The Conference Board.

Figure 1–2. Fifteen Years of Shortfalls in Demand

preceding depression. (The birth forces of a new wave of history should be expected to be of heroic proportions; the federal deficits of 1943 and 1944 amounted to 25 percent of GNP! (See figure 1–3.) The liquidity created during the war was deflated in only small degree by rising prices, since prices (and wages) were subjected to the most effective governmental control in all of history.

To these necessary domestic conditions for a "big bang" and a restarting of economic history should be added the fact that the United States emerged

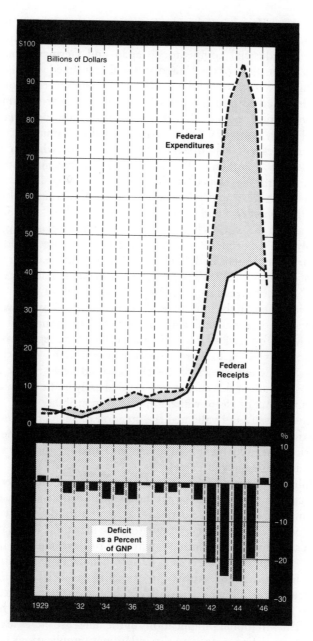

Sources: U.S. Department of Commerce; The Conference Board.

Figure 1–3. The Federal Budget in Depression and War

from World War II in a condition of international economic and technological dominance unsurpassed in the history of any nation anywhere. Its
most effective industrial competitors, Japan and Germany, had suffered
industrial ruin; the allies of the United States also suffered varying degrees of
damage, while U.S. territory and its industrial facilities were untouched. The
United States emerged into the postwar world in a near vacuum of international competition, equipped with the world's only industrial base. Its
currency—the only reserve currency—commanded such immense respect that
for twenty-five years it was preferred to the gold for which it was freely
exchangeable at $35 an ounce. Indeed, the most serious international prob-
lem confronting the developed world after World War II was the threat
that a dollar shortage would inhibit the growth of international trade. The
International Monetary Fund's "special drawing rights," the SDRs, were
invented to add to the world's liquidity at a time when foreign supplies of the
dollar simply could not increase (that is, the United States could not run a
deficit requiring settlement in dollars). The United States ran a trade surplus
in every postwar year until 1971; its first significant deficit on current account
was in 1977; its net investment income reached a peak in 1981.

A final ingredient in the initial energy of this wave of history was a unique
intersection of attitudinal and cultural trends. The trauma of the Great
Depression had produced a violent liberalization of the legislative structure
of the economy, seeking to provide assurance—in many respects, literally
insurance—that the experience of the 1930s would never recur. The philosophical substructure of this change was ratified early in the postwar years by
the Employment Act of 1946, which imposed responsibility for prosperity on
the government itself, and validated the creation of such antirecession, pro-
security institutions (many of them created in skeleton form in the 1930s) as
social security, unemployment compensation, bank deposit guarantees, and
farm debt and mortgage guarantees.

But while the Depression liberalized the structure of the system, it had a
powerfully conservative impact on the behavior of people as consumers and
businessmen. This conservative, risk-averse set of attitudes survived far into
the postwar years, deferring and modulating the inevitable liquidation of the
imposed increase in security through increased risk assumption. It is a valid
principle of economics (valid, even if hard to demonstrate statistically) that
nonmarket increments to security produced by a socioeconomic system
(social security, unemployment insurance, deposit insurance, health insurance, and so forth) will in time be liquidated by lower saving and higher debt
incurrence. The inflationary implications of the immense increase in liquidity
attributable to war financing, and the inflationary implications of the great
social programs installed during the thirties, lay dormant for two decades,
as attitudes toward debt and risk remained strikingly conservative. (For
ten years, the average term on automobile installment credit stayed below
two years.)

To conclude on this spectacular experience, there has never been a more violent rupture of conventional economic relationships than in the fifteen years of U.S. history ending with peace in 1945. The end of World War II marked an explosive release of energy, and a spectacular new dawn for the U.S. economy. The multiple generation of World War II veterans, 15 million strong, that poured into the U.S. labor market in 1945 and 1946 started their careers in the morning light of a great boom.

The Wave in Transit

Mornings do not last forever, and booms consume their energies as they go. Granting the awesome original energy involved, historical tracing of the course of the postwar explosion through time should nevertheless not be expected to be easy, or to reveal a high degree of regularity, periodicity, or a clear continuity of evidence; the underlying history is a complex aggregate of many interweaving forces. It is subject to modifications attributable to the stops and starts of the short-term business cycle, alterations of short-term economic policy, variations in the behavior of other economies with which the United States has trade and financial relationships, and floodtides and then abatements in major domestic markets (for example, the suburbanization nexus of demands for housing, roads, automobiles, and then schools arising out of the postwar elevation of the birthrate).

Developments in all of these more local conditions are described in later chapters. But what appears in the aggregate history is progressive exhaustion of the strengths out of which the wave originated; progressive deteriorations in liquidity and in the debt burden; gradual engagement of, and then increased dependence on, the public insurance programs legislated in the Depression and progressively expanded in the first three postwar decades; increasingly reluctant response of the system to the conventional stimuli provided by economic policy; and gradual—ultimately, total—reversal of the huge resources of economic energy available in the international dominance of the United States in 1945.

The private debt burden would now appear to be mature by almost any criterion. Ratios of debt to the income flows that must service them are high (and still rising) throughout the private sector (see figure 1–4). Defaults and bankruptcies have risen, at least moderately, in the housing market and in installment credit. A violent burst of default has prevailed in the agricultural economy for several years. In the automobile market and in the housing market the term of loans stopped rising several years ago. In earlier stages of the wave, rejuvenation of debt formation was periodically achieved by further lengthening of average terms; terms are now at a practical maximum. (The 1986 tax bill is phasing out the use of installment credit and substituting home-equity debt, which is providing a temporary rejuvenation for markets

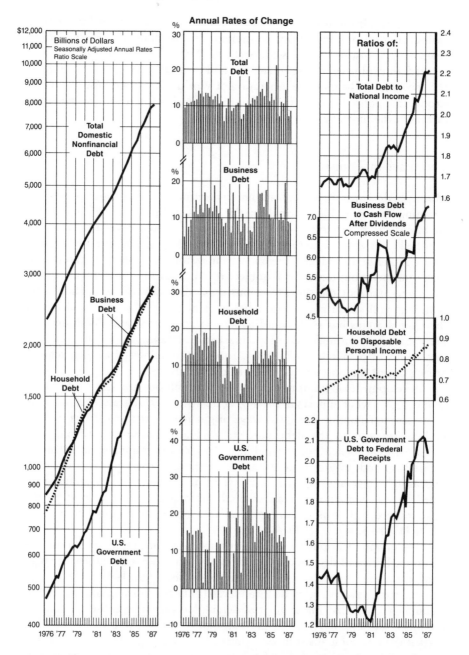

Sources: Federal Reserve Board; U.S. Department of Commerce; The Conference Board.

Figure 1–4. The Maturing of the Debt Burden

dependent on credit.) Characteristically for a period of weak underlying general business conditions, the federal deficit is immense, and the accumulating federal debt is growing rapidly—faster than the growth of aggregate debt, so that the share of federal debt in the total is rising, as it characteristically does during periods of weak business conditions. The ratio of the federal debt to a year's GNP was about 1.0 at the end of war financing in 1946; it fell almost without interruption in the postwar boom, reaching a trough of about .33 in 1981; it has since risen to about .55 in 1987.

The debt burden has been made more onerous by a subdued rate of inflation. Inflation itself was constrained throughout the earlier stages of the wave; it accelerated during the 1970s and began subsiding late in the decade and in the 1980s, mainly for reasons involving currency values and trends in international trade. Whatever else it is, inflation is at least an indication of strong underlying demand and of the dominance of sellers (of labor, as well as of goods) over buyers. The absence of deflation of debt through rising prices and incomes is a compound component of this history. Rapid growth of debt was partly responsible for the inflation; the years 1983–1986 witnessed continuing growth of the debt but no longer with inflationary consequences for prices and incomes. (In 1985 and 1986, the growth rate of both public and private debt was double the growth rate of nominal GNP, and four times the inflation of prices and incomes.) The agricultural sector stands as a gross illustration of the interweaving of the waves of debt and inflation, and of the final position in which debt has moved from stimulus to burden. (A renewed subwave in the course of U.S. inflation, imposed by the devaluation of the dollar, began developing in 1987, but it is not likely to benefit U.S. debtors; see chapter 6).

The so-called velocity of money (the speed at which money turns over) has fallen in the real world of output and income, but it has increased enormously in financial markets, which have experienced vast multiplication of secondary security volume (in mortgage-backed securities, packaged receivables, mutual fund issuance, and so forth) and an accompanying explosion in volume. The great increase in credit availability in the 1980s thus seems to have bypassed the real world, and been absorbed in financial turnover. The so-called high real interest rate that seems to prevail in the U.S. economy reflects this ravenous appetite of the financial sector, at a time when the inflation rate prevailing in the real world has been subdued by sluggish demand. It does not take much imagination or picturesque prose to describe this phenomenon as the consequence of powerful monetary stimulus applied to a tired real world.

The condition of fiscal policy carries the same suggestion of exhaustion. From late 1982 to the end of 1986, a huge budget deficit was accompanied by accommodative monetary policy—a kind of Keynesian shock, vastly smaller, of course, than the shock delivered to the system during World War II, but nevertheless powerful stimulus for a peacetime economy. The same degree of

stimulus delivered to the system two decades ago would have been expected
to produce roaring growth and inflation and, of course, therefore a balanced
budget or a surplus; its reflection now is dim and exhausted. Throughout
the three decades, a federal budget deficit has become less and less self-
correcting; in the late 1980s, the supposed economic stimulus from budget
deficits no longer seems operative at all.

Economic policy has thus already assumed the posture it normally adopts
in periods of serious recession. The money stock has recently grown far faster
than the dollar value of economic activity; expenditure velocity reached a
peak as long ago as 1981. Interest rates have fallen dramatically since their
erratic peaks of 1980–1981 and are back generally to their levels of a decade
ago. The decline in interest rates, in the presence of several conditions suggestive of high rates (a weak currency, a trade deficit, a huge budget deficit,
low aggregate saving), is an indication of how accommodative monetary
policy has been, on the whole, since late 1982. The system's sluggish and
uncertain growth, in response to the massive stimulus of large budget deficits
financed accommodatively, is testimony to the withdrawing underlying tide
in the system.

Finally, the international position of the United States, which was one of
its most extraordinary strengths at the start of the long wave, has reversed
with a vengeance. The U.S. trade position has deteriorated with respect to
virtually all of its geographic markets. Its technology is available around the
world, where it is often associated with labor costs that are a fraction of the
cost level built in the United States through thirty years of an ascendant
boom. Countries whose imports from the United States were largely financed
by rapid growth of loans from the United States can no longer finance the
loans and can no longer import. Our erstwhile enemies, Japan and West
Germany, operating with capital facilities of a much younger average age
than our own, now run in the one instance a large, and in the other instance a
gigantic, trade surplus with the United States. The United States has become
a net borrower in international financial markets, to such a degree that the
entire surplus of investment abroad over foreign investment in the United
States has been wiped out. (See figure 1–5.) At the end of 1986, the net debt
to foreigners exceeded $260 billion, and was still growing at more than $100
billion a year. The net earnings flow achieved by the United States on foreign
investment threatens to disappear entirely.

These changes—in debt position, in liquidity, in inflation, in response to
policy stimulus, in international trade and capital flows—can be viewed as
individual deteriorations, in individual areas. (It can be argued, for example,
that the U.S. trade deficit is even now no more than a delayed and ultimately
reversible consequence of the dollar's rapid rise in 1983–1985.) But
their interconnections are substantial; taken together, viewed as interactive

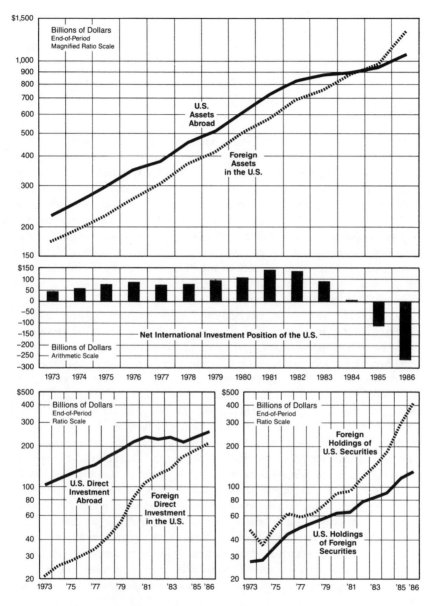

Sources: U.S. Department of Commerce; The Conference Board.

Figure 1–5. The Decline in the U.S. International Investment Position

history, they describe progressive involution of virtually all of the conditions on which the birth of America's unparalleled postwar prosperity rested. Their deterioration has reached a point that suggests that the culmination of the boom, and its inevitable reversal, is now at least a few years in the past, and that the system is now already well into a struggle to offset a cumulative drain on its energies.

Worldview

For nearly a century, the United States has been the indisputable world leader in terms of the size of its domestic markets. In the years after World War II, it was also the world's largest source of capital. The Marshall Plan, and then the awesome wave of U.S. investment in manufacturing facilities in Europe and North America, as well as in energy in the Middle East, and then finally its credit extension to less-developed countries (the LDCs), distributed its assets and influence to almost all parts of the world. It was, truly, the world's locomotive. The United States now shares dominance with a recovered Europe and the surging economies of the Pacific Rim—itself evidence of its changed position in history. But the sheer size of its markets retains for it a crucial position in the world economy.

By the middle of 1986, it was becoming clear that the time of troubles in the United States was beginning to have an impact on other developed economies, at least partly through the consequences of the devaluation of the dollar, but also partly because the downdrift in U.S. economic energy was reducing the role of the world's largest economy as a locomotive. As the effects of the declining dollar have become more visible in Europe and Japan, concern over the sluggish, apparently compromised growth rate of the United States has broadened into a concern that the whole *developed* world (therefore the *whole* world) is in a phase of dwindling economic energy, failing growth rates, and, conceivably, serious international recession. The long wave in the United States has thus spread to the developed world as a whole.

The deteriorated long-term performance of the U.S. economy was bound in time to affect all the other developed economies with which the United States trades heavily. This is true even though the relative success of those other economies (principally, of course, West Germany and Japan) is a major reason why U.S. experience deteriorated. This circularity is typical of economic process: the weakened U.S. market, and its weakened currency, are now arresting the growth of those economies that prospered by exporting to it.

With respect to trade, there is no longer an energized voltage gap within the universe of the developed economies; the weak have grown strong and the strong have weakened. Instead, the energy lies between that universe and the universe of newly industrialized countries (the NICs) equipped with advanced technology but still experiencing far lower labor costs and living standards. The NICs—South Korea, Taiwan, Hong Kong, Malaysia, Brazil, Mexico—constitute a new economic presence out there, an unprecedented combination of high technology and low cost. They are young, vigorous, hungry, unencumbered by high living standards. They grew up largely unobserved in the shadow of the American boom. The evidence of their broad and pervasive invasion into the world of the developed economies is appearing now. Dramatic change in the currency relationships within the developed world is being reflected in dwindling growth among the great exporters, Japan and West Germany, while the trade deficit of the United States, the great importer, is still huge and declining only slowly. In the presence of rapid growth among developing economies, trade outcomes among the developed economies no longer constitute a zero-sum game.

The United States is thus no longer a net contributor of energy to the developed world. The long wave so clearly traceable to the explosion of 1946, and so readily documented through the four-decade trajectory reviewed here, might now be said to have been internationalized, as the United States struggles to support its growth rate, as well as to support a living standard developed in the soaring years of the first postwar quarter-century. The unresponsiveness of the U.S. economy to economic policy stimulus, the extreme rate of growth of foreign debt on the part of the United States, even the rise in interest rates in early 1987 required to support its currency, are evidence that a locomotive role for the United States is no longer possible.

If the generally prosperous condition of the developed world in the years of this history was born in the enlightened exercise of unprecedented dominance by the American economy starting at the end of World War II, then no comparable rebirth seems to be visible on the horizon. This by no means argues that the United States, or the rest of the developed world, faces an unavoidable encounter with deep and prolonged recession. But it does suggest that there are only modest policy opportunities for supporting, and then gradually rebuilding, a universe that has consumed its inherited energies and is struggling to maintain modest growth. The U.S. economy must now live in the present. The lesson of this history is not panic but prudent caution, exercised at least until the new world we have entered reveals more clearly its promises and dangers. The history also suggests that standard reasoning of the past that worked in a period of American supremacy will require constant and careful appraisal to ensure that it still works in a world so greatly altered by the end of an era.

If there is an ultimate caution in this history, it lies in the seeming unwillingness of the United States to recognize its new position, and to act accordingly. The United States cannot hope to return to more vigorous growth until it comes to grips with the passionate dedication to consumption it developed during its decades of world supremacy. Probably the most important contribution the United States can make to its own future, and therefore to the future of the world economy, would be an elevation of its real saving rate — to provide for its own capital requirements by constraining its consumption, thereby freeing resources for export, and for investment at home. The later chapters of this book, dealing with issues of the business cycle, of inflation, of government policies, and of the world environment, make, over and over again, the point of the need for a new national governance in U.S. economic behavior, one that recognizes the realities of the U.S. economic situation in the remainder of this decade. One way of stating the significance of late 1987 (and the concurrent further decline of the dollar) is that it marked a worldwide recognition that an era of dependence on American consumption of the world's output has drawn to a close.

2
The National Economic
Accounting System

The U.S. national accounting system—often referred to simply as the GNP accounts—is a magnificent summary of economic activity in the United States, packed with information for business executives and their advisers. The accounts represent the apex of an immense statistical pyramid provided by public and private agencies engaged in the collection of economic and business statistics. The accounting structure of the national accounts organizes this enormous flow of data under consistent accounting definitions and concepts, and builds them into a coherent portrait of aggregate economic activity. The accounts are available quarterly. Their earliest release, normally about twenty days after the end of a quarter, is a very big statistical event, celebrated and analyzed throughout the business world. Two progressive revisions incorporating more and more detailed knowledge of events appear in the ensuing several weeks. The preliminary release and the later revisions are the best and most complete general portrait of what is happening in all the major sectors of the U.S. economy. In addition, they provide a great statistical skeleton of the history described above, all the way back to 1929. The U.S. national accounts are widely considered to be the best, and most promptly available, economic accounts in the world.

In today's world, in which broad trends in economic activity and policy decisions have prompt and powerful implications for individual markets, a reasonable working knowledge of this accounting system would seem to be as important to the business executive as a working knowledge of business accounting. The national accounts serve the same general purpose—namely, to provide the stockholders (that's us) with a summary overview of the condition and direction of the U.S. economy, viewed as a giant, departmentalized business generating streams of output and streams of income.

The aggregate, summary character of the national accounts has also inevitably made them the principal vehicle of aggregate economic forecasting; the accounts are, in fact, the very language in which general forecasts are couched. Making efficient use of the economic forecasts available, relating them to activities of an individual firm, and drawing from them the prospects for policy variables such as interest rates and taxes, requires a basic understanding of the national accounting system.

This summary description of the national accounts is intended to serve just those purposes—to provide a framework for grasping the significance of each new quarterly set as it makes its appearance in the press, and to provide a basis for comparing actual developments in the economy with those projected by the forecasting fraternity.

In addition to their utility in appraising current and prospective economic conditions, the national accounts represent the statistical universe to which economic policy is applied. Budget estimates of the federal government rest on assumptions with respect to the course of the national economy as described in the national accounts. Monetary policy draws its objectives from the condition of the system, and the relative desirability of stimulus or constraint in the light of present behavior as revealed in the quarterly releases of the national accounts. Sensing the probable course of these important influences on economic activity (and particularly on financial markets) thus also depends on a knowledge of the national accounts.

For all their jargon and the occasional exotic departures from familiar accounting that are required for so complex an economic system, the national accounts stand as the jewel of U.S. statistics. It is difficult to convey the richness of detail available in the total set of accounts; the reader is urged to refer to the annual national-accounts issue of the *Survey of Current Business,* appearing every July (published by the U.S. Department of Commerce), which revise and update the entire system, always carrying the revision back several years on the basis of newly available data.

The Structure of the Accounts

The conceptual structure of the national accounts bears a powerful family resemblance to ordinary accounting. It has its own peculiarities, and its nomenclature is necessarily somewhat special. The accounting principles themselves, however, are on the whole simple, logical, and reasonably familiar; there are peculiarities, but no mysteries. Even the peculiarities are rational responses to the special problems posed by accounting for all the activities of a vast, diversified entity that incorporates governmental as well as private activity and (unlike a private corporation) consumes virtually all of its own output.

The U.S. economy described in these accounts can be thought of as a giant company, employing the whole working population, producing all consumer goods (which it sells in its company store) and all the capital goods it requires for its own production facilities, while providing its employees with incomes and benefits, and borrowing back their savings to invest for the future. To keep a running record of all these activities, the conceptual structure incorporates the following basic principles.

Double-Entry Bookkeeping

The national accounts are a double-entry bookkeeping system, recording the total economic output of the economy on the one hand, and tabulating all the resulting income flows on the other hand.

The total income flows generated by the system—the compensation of employees, the earnings of the self-employed, the earnings from real and financial property—are conceptually equal to the value of the total output (with a few minor qualifications, discussed later). Think of a typical business operating statement: If the net income before taxes is thought of as payment to capital, then total costs (including depreciation) equal total gross revenues (see figure 2–1).

Avoiding Double Counting of Output

The output side of the account is generally restricted to counting the output of finished product.

It would obviously grossly overstate output if the production and sale of intermediate products were included in the total. For example, if we count the steel (produced by a steel company) and *then* count the automobiles (produced by an automobile producer) that incorporate the steel, we would be counting the steel twice. The value of the steel is embedded in the value of the car.

This method of adding is equivalent to summing up the *value added* at each level of production—that is, the wage costs, capital costs (including profit), and depreciation costs experienced by the seller and embedded in the selling price. For each seller, it is the equivalent of sales, less costs on purchases from others. Intermediate purchases thus wash out of the total. The one exception to this count is in the treatment of inventory. Production of steel that appears as an *increase* in steel inventories held by producers and consumers of steel must be counted as output; here, double counting is avoided since the steel has not yet been sold in a final product. Increases in *all* inventory (including such finished products as automobiles in dealer stocks) are included in the sum of output.

Output Is Valued at Market

The accounts value the physical outputs at market prices—that is, at their sales price.

A special condition arises here because not all output actually passes through a market. An easy illustration is food produced on a farm but

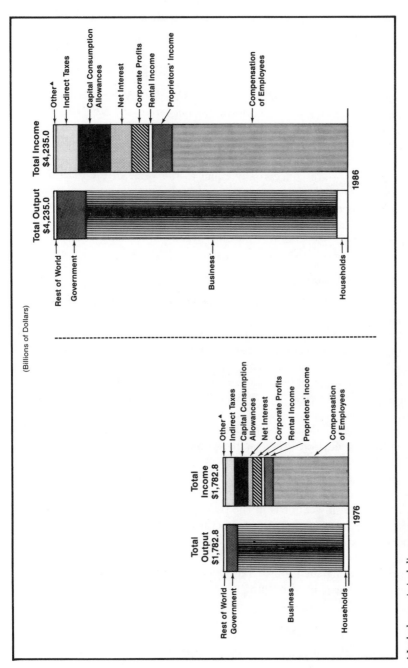

(Billions of Dollars)

▲ Includes statistical discrepancy.

Sources: U.S. Department of Commerce; The Conference Board.

Figure 2–1. Output Equals Income

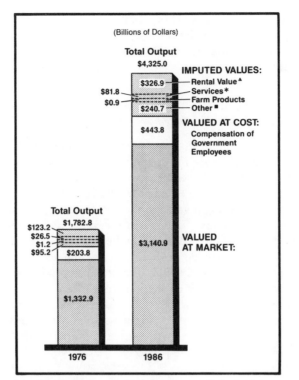

(Billions of Dollars)

Total Output
$4,325.0

IMPUTED VALUES:
Rental Value ▲
Services *
Farm Products
Other ■

VALUED AT COST:
Compensation of Government Employees

VALUED AT MARKET:

$326.9
$81.8
$0.9
$240.7
$443.8
$3,140.9

Total Output
$1,782.8
$123.2
$26.5
$1.2
$95.2
$203.8
$1,332.9

1976   1986

▲ Includes farm and nonfarm housing, rental values of nonprofit institutions.

*By financial intermediaries, except life insurance carriers.

■ Includes employee-related food, clothing, and shelter; and miscellaneous housing and equipment.

Sources: U.S. Department of Commerce; The Conference Board.

Figure 2–2. Value of Output

consumed by the farm family. In this instance, the accounts estimate the market value and add it to the *output* (and to the *income,* and to the *expenditures*) of farm households. Such estimates are called *imputed income* and *imputed expenditure.* Other, more complicated forms of this problem appear in the housing industry (discussed later in this chapter). Government output (mostly services performed by government employees) is generally valued at its cost to the government, but the great bulk of output is valued at a market price (see figure 2–2).

The GNP Is Gross

The total output of the system is usually referred to simply as GNP—**gross national product.** The term *gross* is required because the aggregate does not make a deduction for the exhaustion of capital in producing the output—*that is, it is before a depreciation deduction.* (In national accounting, depreciation is referred to as **capital consumption allowances.**) In addition to ordinary business assets, the accounts also treat residential properties as depreciable assets.

Capital Gains and Losses Excluded

It should be borne in mind that the national accounts are a purified set of statistics—*purified to remove the creation or destruction of values that have nothing to do with actual output or income earned in the accounting period.* A rise in the price level would elevate the value of a constant stock of inventory. As noted, this increased valuation, not representing output, is excluded from the national accounts. Changes in the value of existing assets of all types, real and financial, are excluded on the same grounds. All transactions in existing assets are excluded on both sides of the account; for corporate profits, as well as for personal income, capital gains and losses are excluded (where necessary, removed by estimation from subsidiary data that may include them). Income from existing assets—for example, interest payments—*is* included, as representing the current services performed by financial capital; similarly, rental income represents the market value of the current services performed by a rentable property.

GNP Includes Goods, Services, and Construction

The measure of output includes all forms of output—not simply tangible goods, but also creation of new construction and output of services.

The output side of the national accounts, by type of output, is shown for recent years in figure 2–3.

Output Equals Demand

The total output of the economic system is exactly equal to the total demand in the system; in fact, gross national product can also be referred to as gross national expenditure.

A moment's thought reveals that this is not a matter of divine intervention. *The holdings of inventory in the system are treated as a repository for output.* If actual **final demand** in the system were to fall short of actual output, inventories would necessarily rise, and the expenditure for inventory would be a reconciling positive number. Conversely, if final demand were to exceed output, the result would be a decline in inventory (a negative demand), reconciling the two aspects of the accounts. An increase in inventories is not, of course, always exactly voluntary. Whether voluntary or not,

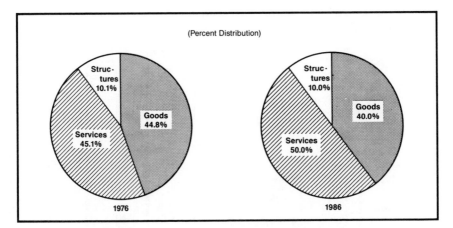

(Percent Distribution)

1976

Struc- tures 10.1%

Goods 44.8%

Services 45.1%

1986

Struc- tures 10.0%

Goods 40.0%

Services 50.0%

Sources: U.S. Department of Commerce; The Conference Board.

Figure 2–3. Output, by Type

a rise in inventories is treated as a *demand* or *expenditure* for inventory; a decline in inventory is a *negative demand*. There is no inventory of services; they are consumed in the instant of their performance, and output of services always exactly equals demand. There is also no inventory of unfinished construction; the accounts pick up as fixed investment all on-site activity, whether or not the structure is finished (see figure 2–4).

Output and Demand by Sector

One way of slicing up the nation's aggregate output and expenditure is by *sector*—that is, *output and expenditure by government, by households, by business, and by our so-called international sector.*

Obviously, the identity of output and expenditure does not apply at the level of the individual sector. Only a small portion of total output is generated by households, but households take the bulk of the output off the market. It might be said that the household sector *imports* product from the other sectors. The government sector also uses up more resources than it produces. Conversely, business creates far more output than it consumes (both in growth of inventory and in growth of its capital account); it *exports* to the other sectors. In our relations with the rest of the world, our international sector is sometimes a net exporter and sometimes a net importer. When the four sectors are added together, the identity of aggregate output and aggregate expenditure is restored. Figure 2–5 shows the output and expenditure of the sectors, and of the total economy, in recent years.

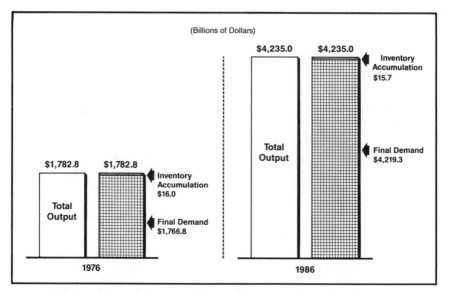

Sources: U.S. Department of Commerce; The Conference Board.

Figure 2–4. Output Equals Demand

Total Expenditure Equals Total Income

If total output *equals both total expenditure and total income, then total expenditure equals total income.*

This identity applies to the economy as a whole but not to individual sectors of the economy. Typically, the consumer sector spends *less* than its income; that is, it is a net *saver.* The business sector typically spends *more* than its income; that is, it is a net *investor. Viewed this way, total saving in the economy equals total investment — an accounting identity that has many uses* (discussed later in this chapter).

Who Takes How Much of the Output

Although the aggregate is normally referred to as a product rather than an expenditure, the most frequently published structure of the outputs is by expenditure totals, rather than by output totals.

The common releases on the GNP break the aggregate down into (1) the amount of GNP taken off the market by households and individuals (personal consumption expenditures); (2) the portion taken off the market by business itself (gross private domestic investment, including investment in inventory); (3) the part that *on balance* has been shipped abroad — exports

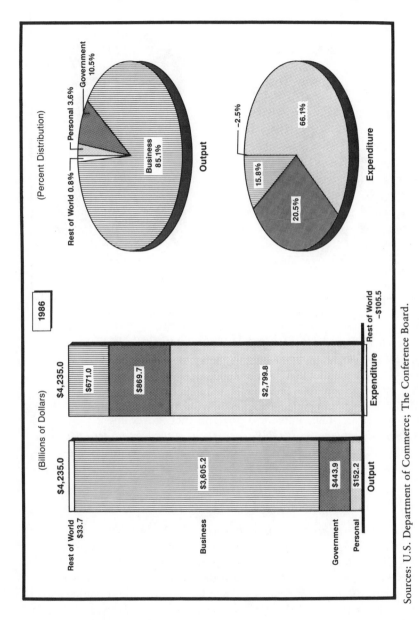

Sources: U.S. Department of Commerce; The Conference Board.

Figure 2–5. Output and Expenditure, by Sector

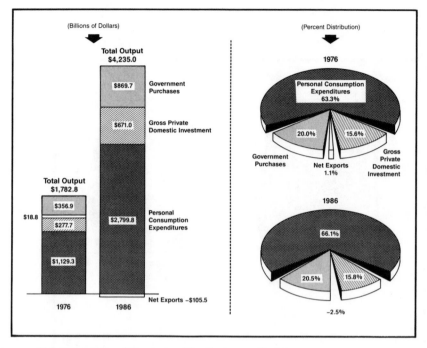

Sources: U.S. Department of Commerce; The Conference Board.

Figure 2–6. Who Takes How Much of the Output

minus imports, or *net exports;* and (4) the portion of the output taken off the market by federal, state, and local governments (government purchases). *This is the basic table in most GNP forecasts; it is the first target of the forecasting models.* The composition of these outlays, by sector, is shown for recent years in figure 2–6.

Price and Physical Output in GNP

In the usual form in which it is published, GNP is expressed in current prices—that is, the price level prevailing in the accounting period.

Thus GNP will change as prices change and output levels change. In this form, GNP is *price × output;* every recorded change in GNP is nonspecific with respect to the measurement of change in output alone, or price alone. To permit this separation, the U.S. Department of Commerce obligingly produces a separate measure of the change in the *physical output,* and a separate measure of the change in the *price level.* The output change describes the real growth (or decline) of the system as a whole; the change in the price index records the degree of inflation (or, very rarely indeed, deflation) of the system as a whole.

The value of the GNP *before* correction for prices is often called current-dollar GNP, or **nominal GNP.** The GNP *after* correction for price change is called *real GNP,* or *constant-dollar GNP,* or *GNP in 1982 prices.* The last term arises because **real GNP** is now constructed by pricing all output, in *all* years, at the price level prevailing in 1982, thus removing price change from any period-to-period movement in this series.

If *nominal* GNP is divided by *real* GNP, the result is an index of price change, with a base of 1982 equal to 100. Because this price index is not constructed by the usual method of combining component price indexes directly through a weighting system (as with the consumer price index) it is often called the **implicit price deflator.** The deflator is generally considered the best measure of the aggregate inflation rate.

The arithmetic of all of this is as follows:

$$\frac{\text{Nominal GNP}}{\text{Real GNP}} = \frac{\text{Quantity} \times \text{Current Price}}{\text{Quantity} \times \text{1982 Price}} =$$

$$\frac{\text{Current Price}}{\text{1982 Price}} = \text{Price Index, } 1982 = 100$$

Figure 2–7 shows the change in output in recent years, the change in the price level in those years, and the change in the aggregate GNP itself.

GNP Level and GNP Change

The *definitions* of output and income exert a powerful influence on the size of the GNP and of the related income flows. What should be treated as economic output? For example, the efforts of housewives in managing their homes are ignored in the national accounts; their work is not valued in the GNP, nor is there an imputed income to their families from their services. Inclusion of their efforts (through imputation, as with food consumed on the farm) would substantially elevate both the gross national product and (in exactly the same amount) the flow of income to the household sector. Because this component of the system is ignored, the entry of a housewife into the work force elevates the GNP, with no corresponding offset for the loss of activity at home. In fact, if the household so deprived of its manager were to turn to commercial services, such as a commercial laundry, the GNP (and national income) would be further elevated. *The inclusiveness of the definition affects the level of the gross national product. Its change from year to year and quarter to quarter, resting on a consistent definition over time, is relatively free of this problem, and carries a much higher significance than the actual dollar levels.*

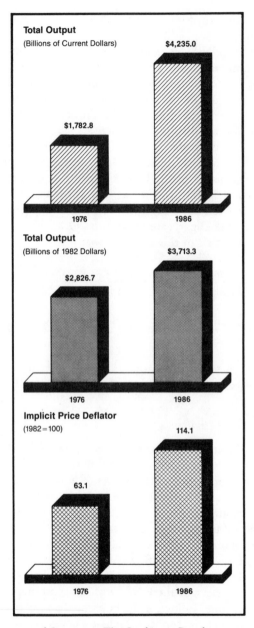

Total Output
(Billions of Current Dollars)
$4,235.0
$1,782.8
1976   1986

Total Output
(Billions of 1982 Dollars)
$3,713.3
$2,826.7
1976   1986

Implicit Price Deflator
(1982=100)
114.1
63.1
1976   1986

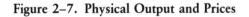

Sources: U.S. Department of Commerce; The Conference Board.

Figure 2–7. Physical Output and Prices

Table 2-1
Calculation of Quarterly Rates of Change in Total Output
(dollar figures in billions)

	1986 III Quarter	1986 IV Quarter	Quarterly Rates of Change	Annual Rates of Change
1. Unadjusted Quarterly Total	$1,068.9	$1,105.7		
2. Seasonal Adjustment Factor	100.2	103.1		
3. Adjusted Quarterly Total	1,066.5	1,072.0		
4. Adjusted Quarterly Total, Annualized	4,265.9	4,288.1		
5. Quarter-to-Quarter Rate of Change			+0.5%	
6. Quarter-to-Quarter Annual Rate of Change, Compounded				+2.1%
A. Adjusted Quarterly Total, Annualized	$4,265.9	$4,288.1	+0.5%	+2.1%
B. Implicit Price Deflator, 1982 = 100	114.7	114.9	+0.2%	+0.7%
C. Real (1982 Dollar) Adjusted Quarterly Total, Annualized . .	$3,718.0	$3,731.5	+0.4%	+1.5%

Sources: U.S. Department of Commerce; The Conference Board.

A Necessary Statistical Note

The annual figures in the national accounts are, of course, annual totals for the specified activity or income flow—the accumulated total for the calendar year. The *quarterly* figures in the national accounts undergo two statistical processes that make them comparable to the levels of the annual data (see table 2-1).

The first of these is a *seasonal adjustment* done to all the components of the total, which corrects the particular *quarterly* figure for normal seasonal occurrences during the quarter. For example, housing-construction activity rises rapidly in the second calendar quarter of every year, not because of an actual change in conditions in the industry, but because such a rise is a normal seasonal reflection of improved weather conditions for construction activity. Similarly, sales of automobiles rise seasonally in the second quarter, and sales of refrigerators and air conditioners in the third quarter. Total retail sales reach a minor climax around Easter, and a major climax before Christmas. To the extent that the changes in the components simply reflect normal seasonal behavior, they are corrected by seasonal adjustment.

After the figures are adjusted for seasonal conditions, the quarterly figures are multiplied by four to elevate the adjusted quarterly totals to an *annual rate*. The abbreviation *SAAR*, which often appears in the headings of tables showing national-accounts data, indicates that the quarterly figures are at *seasonally adjusted annual rates.* The advantage of these processes is that they put the quarterly data for the national accounts at levels that are comparable to the annual data, thereby permitting useful comparisons—for example, "The annual *rate* of general economic activity in the second quarter of 1983 is back to the rate prevailing in 1979." These procedures are pursued throughout the accounts: All the output components, as well as expenditures and income flows, are published on a SAAR basis.

A percentage change from one quarter to the next in any of the SAAR national-accounts figures is nevertheless still only a quarterly change. It is often useful to put the changes themselves at a *compounded annual rate,* which requires raising the change to a fourth power. From the fourth quarter of 1986 to the first quarter of 1987, total national output, in current dollars, rose 1.9 percent; it was rising at an *annual* rate of 1.019 to the fourth power (1.019^4), or 7.6 percent. *The real growth rate in the national accounts for any quarter*—a very widely reported figure, generally taken to be an indication of how well or poorly real economic activity is progressing—is the quarter-to-quarter change in real output (adjusted for inflation), raised to the fourth power (compounded) to indicate the degree of improvement that would be achieved over an entire year if the improvement continued for four quarters at that particular quarterly rate. Similarly, the most widely reported inflation rate for the system is the quarter-to-quarter change in the *implicit price index,* raised to an annual inflation rate by compounding.

The figures in the national accounts that find their way to the general reader through the press have thus undergone a great deal of processing, but it is all essentially understandable arithmetic. For the fourth quarter of 1986, it was reported that the real growth rate of the U.S. economy was 1.5 percent, and the inflation rate was 0.7 percent. The calculation of this figure from the raw data is shown in table 2–1.

The Measure of Output and Expenditure

The most-used table in the national accounts shows total expenditure divided by sector and subdivided into kind of product bought. This summary table, together with far more detailed subsidiary tables in the national accounts, describes the behavior of all the markets for product categories, both in the course of the short-term business cycle and over the long term. It is basic information on the trend of business markets (see figure 2–8 and table 2–2).

Personal Consumption Expenditures

Personal consumption expenditures for durable goods, nondurable goods, and services represents the spending—the purchasing of goods and services—

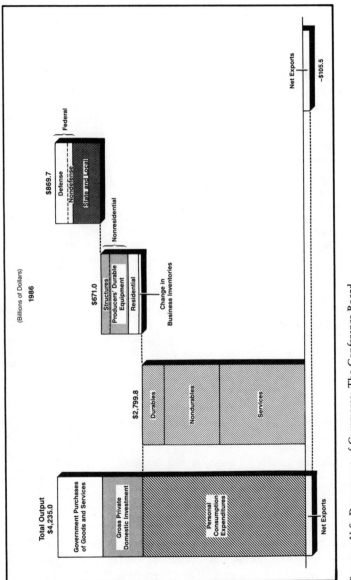

Sources: U.S. Department of Commerce; The Conference Board.

Figure 2–8. Expenditure, by Sector

Table 2–2
Gross National Product Expenditures, by Sector
(dollar figures in billions)

	1984	1985	1986
1. Gross National Product	**$3,772.2**	**$4,010.3**	**$4,235.0**
2. Personal Consumption Expenditures	**2,430.5**	**2,629.4**	**2,799.8**
3. Durables	335.5	368.7	402.4
4. Nondurables	867.3	913.1	939.4
5. Services	1,227.6	1,347.5	1,458.0
6. Gross Private Domestic Investment	**664.8**	**641.6**	**671.0**
7. Residential	181.1	189.0	218.3
8. Nonresidential	416.0	442.6	436.9
9. Structures	141.1	152.5	137.4
10. Producers' Durable Equipment .	274.9	290.1	299.5
11. Change in Business Inventories ..	67.7	10.0	15.7
12. Nonfarm	60.5	13.6	16.8
13. Change in Book Value	66.3	14.3	10.3
14. Inventory Valuation Adjustment	–5.8	–0.7	6.5
15. Farm	7.1	–3.6	–1.1
16. Net Exports of Goods and Services	**–58.9**	**–79.2**	**–105.5**
17. Exports	383.5	369.9	376.2
18. Imports	442.4	449.2	481.7
19. Government Purchases of Goods and Services	**735.9**	**818.6**	**869.7**
20. Federal	310.5	353.9	366.2
21. National Defense	234.3	259.3	277.8
22. Nondefense.................	76.2	94.6	88.4
23. State and Local	425.3	464.7	503.5

Sources: U.S. Department of Commerce; The Conference Board.

of individuals and households. This is by far the largest sectoral market of the GNP, taking between 60 and 65 percent of all output (see figure 2–9).

Expenditures for durable goods include outlays for all goods with a presumed life of more than a year. The component labeled *automobiles and parts* includes all new passenger cars purchased during the accounting period, and net acquisitions (purchases less trade-ins) of all used cars, as well as parts and accessories. Since they represent personal outlay, purchases of imported cars also appear in this category even though they do not involve output of

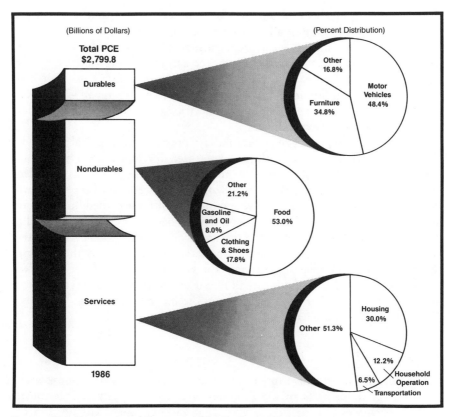

Sources: U.S. Department of Commerce; The Conference Board.

Figure 2–9. Personal Consumption Expenditures, by Type

the U.S. economy. (This first-round overstatement of output is adjusted for, in net exports, to be discussed later.) The durables category also includes all home furnishings, appliances, radio and television sets, books (but not newspapers and magazines), and even some toys. *All outlays of this sector are treated as consumption, none as investment.* Even an automobile, whose average life qualifies it as a depreciable investment if it is bought by a business, is defined as a consumption outlay when it is bought by an individual. This is a definitional matter; the accounts choose to restrict the term *investment* to productive facilities. There is, of course, a *stock* of long-lived consumer durables. In its flow-of-funds data (see chapter 3) the Federal Reserve even calculates an *exhaustion* or *depreciation* factor against this stock; the national accounts do not.

The purchase of nondurables by consumers includes all food and drink (consumed at home or in restaurants), all apparel, gasoline and oil for automobiles and home heating, all medical supplies, and sundries.

Service outlays include all services consumed by households. The largest components are rents, medical outlays, recreational-service outlays, repair services, and personal-care services. Personal-transportation costs — air and railroad fares, fees for local transportation, automotive repair — make up another major component. Outlays for electric, gas, and telephone utilities are treated as service expenditures.

The rental component of service outlays presents some special problems for which rather complicated solutions have been developed. For a household renting its home, no problem arises; the rent represents the services provided by the existing facility, and is included. The existence of owned homes presents a problem, however. If the rental value of these owned homes were excluded from the GNP, the GNP would rise whenever a homeowner sold a home and moved into a rental facility, and would shrink whenever a renter acquired a home. To reflect properly the services performed by the housing stock, the national accounts estimate the rental value of owner-occupied homes, and treat that as a measure of rental-service purchases. Treating rent this way creates further complications on the income side of the accounts, discussed later in this chapter.

Gross Private Domestic Investment

Gross private domestic investment, the second major component of expenditure, covers those parts of the economy that are of a private-investment nature. Each word in the title is significant and necessary. The investment activities measured here are *gross* in the sense that they are *before* any deduction for depreciation. They are *private* because the investment of government is not included. They are *domestic* because they incorporate investment outlays only within the United States. They are *investment* in the ordinary business sense that they are long-lived, depreciable assets — additions to balance sheets (see figure 2–10).

The figure for **residential construction** represents the value of on-site construction activity, of multiple dwellings (garden apartments and apartment houses), and naturally of single-family homes. (Mobile homes are also accounted for as residential construction, even though they are a manufactured product). Included are all outlays during the accounting period — not just for homes and apartments completed during the period, but also for ongoing progress toward completion of structures that will be going on the market in a later accounting period. The figure is not equivalent to a sales value for residential construction; the figure picks up the outlay whether the unit is sold or not, and whether or not the unit is still in the inventory of a home builder. Because all the output of homes is represented in this figure,

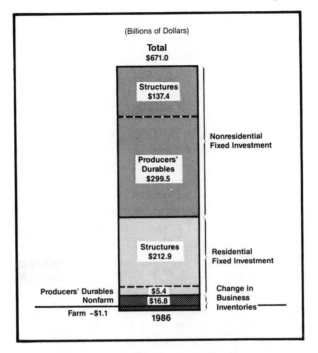

Sources: U.S. Department of Commerce; The Conference Board.

Figure 2–10. Investment Components

the national accounts do not carry an inventory of unsold residential buildings. (Such an inventory figure is available in other data of the U.S. Department of Commerce.) The purchase of a home by a consumer is *not* a consumption expenditure, but is treated as a business investment, putting the buyer in the business of owning a home (discussed later in this chapter).

A second class of investment involves business investment in *plant and equipment.* The plant portion of this total is described in the national accounts as **nonresidential construction,** which includes all such structures — office buildings, manufacturing facilities, warehouses, shopping centers and other retail facilities, and so on. The machinery purchases of the business sector — called **producer durables,** as distinguished from consumer durables — include outlays for all machinery for which depreciation schedules are set up — that is, all machinery and equipment with a life of a year or more. Business purchases of machinery include purchases of automobiles (about one-sixth of all cars sold annually) and trucks.

A final component of gross private domestic investment is called **change in business inventories.** For this component, some simple but special accounting arrangements are required. The intention here is to reflect the *physical increase* or *decrease* in inventories, valued at prevailing prices. At a time of rising prices, the inventories held throughout the business system tend to rise in value, even in the absence of any change in the physical stock of inventory. Ordinary dollar measures on the holdings of business inventories would thus tend to overstate the flow of output into inventory. This would not be true if all U.S. business did its accounting on the basis of LIFO (last in, first out), but a majority of firms continue to use FIFO (first in, first out). These conditions require a correction if the inventory line of the national accounts is to treat inventory as *a repository for actual output,* and if capital gains are to be excluded (as they should be) from output (see figure 1–11).

To resolve this dilemma, the U.S. Department of Commerce adjusts the dollar inventories reported to it by business for an inflation factor; that is, it converts all the inventories in the system to a LIFO basis through an **inventory valuation adjustment,** or *IVA*.

For example, suppose that a company holds 1,000 pounds of copper in inventory, and that its real inventory of copper is unchanged throughout an accounting period in which the market price of copper rises from 60 cents to 70 cents a pound. In the course of the accounting period, it will charge its use of copper in its operating statement at 60 cents a pound if it is on FIFO accounting, but it will be replacing its copper inventory at 70 cents a pound. The book value of its copper inventory will thus rise by 10 cents per pound, even though no *physical* change in its inventory holding has occurred. Through the inventory valuation adjustment, the U.S. Department of Commerce removes this inflation effect from its count of inventory. Since it is after not the dollar level of inventory itself but the *change* in inventory level during the accounting period, it will report a zero change.

As with the special treatment of rental outlay, this treatment of inventory has implications for the income side of the account. *In effect, the inventory valuation adjustment becomes a measure of inventory profit on the income side of the account.* The overvaluation of inventory at the end of the accounting period represents an undercharging of business operating statements for the copper used during the accounting period. Placing business inventories on a replacement-cost basis thus reduces corporate earnings of companies accounting on a FIFO basis in a period of rising prices, and raises them during periods (rare in recent history, but actually occurring in some quarters of 1986) of falling prices (discussed later in this chapter and in chapter 3).

Net Exports

The next major line of the national accounts refers to **net exports.** Here, too, some simple departures from conventional business accounting are required (see figure 2–12). The term *net* in the title of the line reflects the fact that

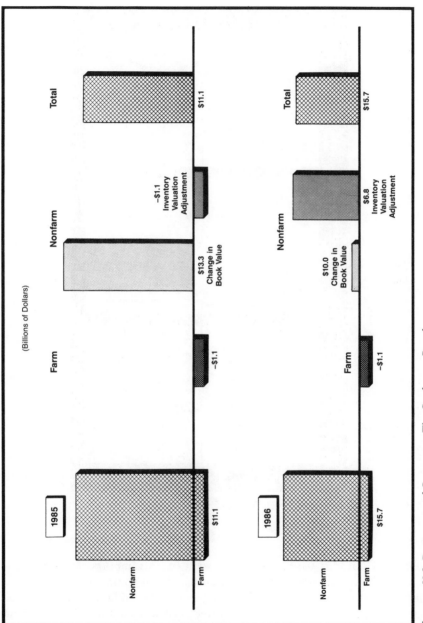

Sources: U.S. Department of Commerce; The Conference Board.

Figure 2–11. Accounting for Inventory Demand

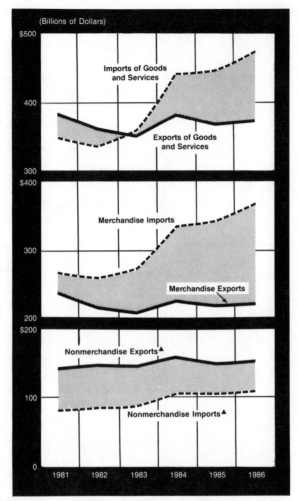

Sources: U.S. Department of Commerce; The Conference Board.

Figure 2–12. Net Exports

what is required is a measure of U.S. exports, less imports. As an illustration, the importation and then the domestic sale of an imported automobile must be picked up in the national accounts if the expenditure totals are to be correct. When the automobile is imported and placed in the inventory of the importer, it becomes a credit to inventory (at the importer's cost); when it is sold to a consumer, the inventory account is debited for its disappearance, and consumer spending for durable goods picks it up as a credit (at its retail sale price). The value of the automobile has moved from one line of the accounts to another, but it is still reflected in the total. Since it is not part of U.S. output and hence cannot be included in the total for GNP, a negative adjustment is required; the adjustment appears as a negative entry (at import cost) under net exports. *In other words, imports find their way into their actual market destination in the national accounts and then are removed from the total in the net export line.* The exports themselves, of course, are part of U.S. output and are properly included in the GNP.

In addition to merchandise trade, the net export line must also reflect the trade in *invisibles.* The principal invisibles are investment income—that is, the earnings of U.S. citizens' investment abroad (whether repatriated to the United States or not)—and tourism. Here, too, the account must be net—that is, tourism outlays of foreigners in the United States less tourism outlays of U.S. citizens abroad, and U.S. earnings from investment abroad less the investment earnings of others in the United States. The net exports line in the national accounts is conceptually close to, but not identical with, the *current account balance* that appears in balance-of-payments statistics. Actual movements of capital into and out of the country, unaccompanied by real expenditure, are transfers of assets and are not reflected in the national accounts.

Government Purchases

Finally, the expenditure of *all levels of government* is a major component of the GNP (see figure 2–13). As it appears in these accounts, federal outlay is divided into national defense and nondefense, the latter category including all **purchases of goods and services** for general government and the operations of all governmental departments. Purchase of the services of government employees—the wage and salary payroll—is included, of course. Net increases in the inventory of crops held by the CCC (Commodity Credit Corporation) are treated as expenditures, and reduction of crop inventory as sales and hence as offsetting income. (The federal government runs no capital account, either within the national accounts or as a part of its own budgetary accounting system.)

The government expenditures in the GNP are limited to purchases of goods and services; they exclude all so-called **transfer payments**—that is, payments made by government but not in return for goods and services. Social security payments and unemployment compensation payments are thus excluded, along with all welfare-type outlays. **Grants-in-aid to state and local governments** are excluded on the same grounds. Mainly by convention, interest payments on the federal debt are treated as transfer payments and, accordingly, are excluded from government purchases of goods and services (see the description of *total* federal budget operations later in this chapter). Expenditures of state and local governments follow the same concepts.

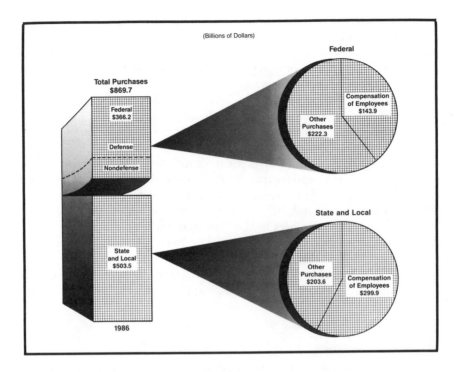

Sources: U.S. Department of Commerce; The Conference Board.

Figure 2–13. Government Expenditures in the National Accounts

The Income Side of the Accounts

Gross national product measures the market value of national output. The income side of the national accounts states the income flows generated in the course of producing the GNP—the income returns to the *factors of production* responsible for the output. These include labor and capital—capital in the fixed form of investment in plant and equipment and residential structures, as well as in the form of property and financial investments that produce rent and interest income.

National Income

The measured flows in **national income** are thus the compensation of employees; the earnings of the self-employed (both including fringe benefits, whether or not in cash); and *property incomes*—profits, rental incomes, and interest incomes. The so-called *national income* is the sum of all these incomes, as GNP itself is the sum of all the outputs. With two important adjustments for conceptual reasons, the two totals of output and income are equal quantities, differing only by a *statistical discrepancy*—a measurement error that separates the output and income sides of the accounts.

The broad identity of the national income with the value of national output is the same old accounting truism: All the costs, including the profits that are the residual return to capital, equal the sales volume. However, some of the costs entering into the gross value of output are not really earned income to a factor of production, and the national income total therefore runs below the value of GNP. (A reconciliation of these series appears in table 2–3; figure 2–1 reconciles the GNP with national income.)

The depreciation flow, though not an earned income, is embedded in the gross national product (which is *gross*, as the reader will recall, precisely *because* it is measured *before* a deduction for depreciation). As a step

Table 2–3
The Reconciliation of GNP with National Income and Personal Income
(billions of dollars)

	1986
1. **Gross National Product**	**$4,235.0**
2. Less: Capital consumption allowances with capital consumption adjustment	456.7
3. Capital consumption allowances without capital consumption adjustment	477.7
4. Less: Capital consumption	21.0
5. **Equals: Net National Product**	**3,778.4**
6. Less: Indirect business tax and nontax liability	347.7
7. Business transfer payments	22.3
8. Statistical discrepancy	–4.9
9. Plus: Subsidies less current surplus of government enterprises	8.7
10. **Equals: National Income**	**3,422.0**
11. Less: Corporate profits with inventory valuation and capital consumption adjustments	284.4
12. Net interest	326.1
13. Contributions for social insurance	374.3
14. Wage accruals less disbursements	0.0
15. Plus: Government transfer payments to persons	496.0
16. Personal interest income	497.6
17. Personal dividend income	81.2
18. Business transfer payments	22.3
19. **Equals: Personal Income**	**3,534.3**

Sources: U.S. Department of Commerce; The Conference Board.

in reconciling the output measure with the income side, GNP must thus be reduced by a measure of capital consumption. This produces a figure called **net national product.** One might think that such a figure would be very useful, representing as it does the flow of goods and services available to the economy *after* the replacement of the capital consumed. The measure of consumed capital is so weak, however, that the concept of net national product is rarely referred to and rarely appears in forecasts.

In addition to the adjustment for capital consumption, it is also necessary to remove from the output side of the accounts the indirect taxes—that is, sales and excise taxes levied at all levels of government. These taxes are embedded in the market value of output, but they are not an earned income flow. (The flows of general tax income to government—from corporate and personal taxes—are included in the national income, but they are not segregated; that is, the private incomes are shown *before* tax.)

These are the major adjustments required to reconcile the income side of the accounts, defined as national income, with the output side. (Two minor adjustments involve net subsidies to government enterprises, and business transfers to individuals of other than earned income.)

The *national income* total is a necessary conceptual counterpart to the GNP, but it is rarely used in analysis and rarely treated in the business press when the figure is released. (Forecasters, almost without exception, simply pass it by.)

Personal Income

The measure of **personal income,** which is available monthly, is a much more effective measure of actual income flows to the personal sector—flows available for personal spending and personal saving. Personal income includes, of course, all the flows of employee compensation that appear in the national income. It also incorporates flows of transfer payments, which are not earned income (and therefore are not reflected in national income or in the GNP measure of government spending) but are nevertheless available for spending and saving. Furthermore, it includes only the dividend flow of income from the corporate sector; that is, it excludes the retained earnings (and the corporate tax liabilities) that are incorporated in the national income total. The monthly appearance of the personal income figure is widely reported, as the best available monthly measure of incomes bearing on retail trade and consumer goods industries. Table 2–3 shows the reconciliation of personal income with national income; figure 2–14 shows the trend of various components of personal income in recent years.

Unlike national income, the resulting figure for personal income is not a pure income measure; it contains a cash-flow component, in the form of the transfers. It is not a pure cash-flow concept either, however, since it excludes, for example, realizations of capital gains and losses in financial markets, and does not reflect the borrowings or repayments of financial obligations.

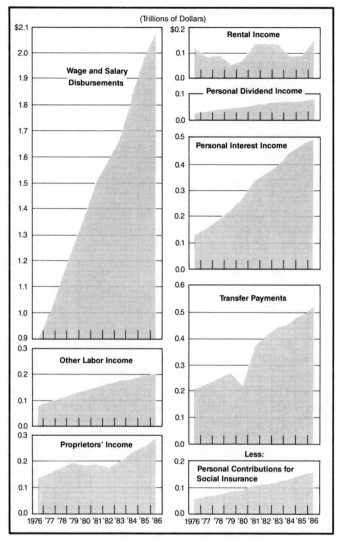

Figure 2–14. Components of Personal Income

Statistics on these excluded flows are broadly available, and for analytical purposes it is often desirable to consider them. (For example, appraisal of the actual net-worth position of the consumer sector in the years 1983 to 1987 had to give weight to very large capital gains and then immense losses, realized or unrealized, in the securities markets.)

Corporate Profits

The **corporate-profits** account in the national income total also receives very wide attention, independently of the release of the national income totals themselves. Unlike the personal-income figure, which undergoes several transformations from the total that appears in the national accounts for employee compensation, the most widely used corporate-profits figures are taken directly from the national accounts, but many useful things can be done to them to increase their significance. Like all the income flows in the national income, the corporate-profits figure is before taxes, but an associated figure reveals the tax liabilities against the income (in the national accounts, the corporate sector's taxes are treated on an accrual basis—that is, as the liability arises—rather than on a payment basis). The after-tax earnings are then subdivided into a component for dividend payments and a component for retained earnings.

Two further adjustments of the aggregate profits-before-taxes figures also appear in the national accounts (see figure 2–15):

1. The inventory profits resulting from appreciation of the existing stock of corporate inventories are removed from the profits figure. It will be recalled that an inventory valuation adjustment is used to remove the effects of price change from the GNP measure of inventory change. In the GNP account, the IVA reflects adjustments for *all* inventories, including those held by unincorporated business. Here the adjustment is calculated only for inventories held by corporations.

2. The U.S. Department of Commerce estimates the presumed actual exhaustion of capital by corporations during the accounting period. If the charges to depreciation accounts by corporations fall short of the actual or true depreciation, the earnings are considered to be overstated by the inadequate provision of depreciation in the corporate operating statement, and the amount of the overstatement is removed from corporate earnings in the form of a **capital-consumption adjustment.** Since the legislation of the accelerated cost recovery system, tax-based depreciation has risen progressively above the U.S. Department of Commerce estimate of true capital exhaustion, and the department is now busily adding back the overdepreciation to corporate earnings (see figure 2–16). These adjustments convert the corporate-profits figures as reported for tax purposes into a figure the U.S. Department of Commerce calls *profits from current production,* which it takes to be a true measure of the ongoing before-tax earnings from operations. If the two adjust-

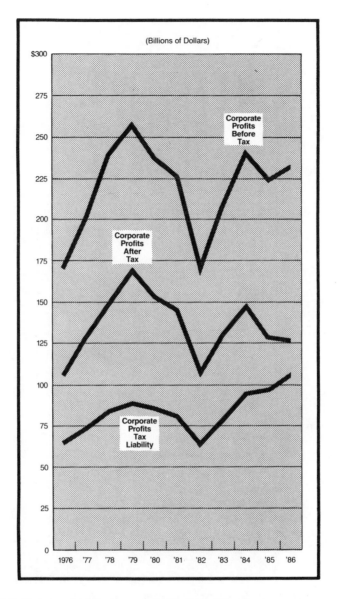

Figure 2–15. Tax-Based Profits in the National Accounts

ments are made to *after-tax* profits, the resulting adjusted series is a better measure of real earnings available for dividends and retained earnings (see figure 2–17). It should be borne in mind that the profits

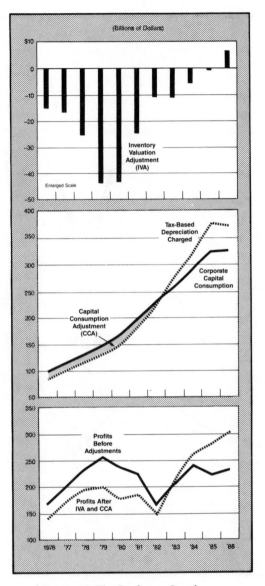

Sources: U.S. Department of Commerce; The Conference Board.

Figure 2–16. Adjustments to Corporate Profits before Taxes

accounts within the national accounts, in common with all the other components, is free of all capital gains and losses. It includes earnings of U.S. corporations from investments all over the world, whether or not all the earnings are repatriated.

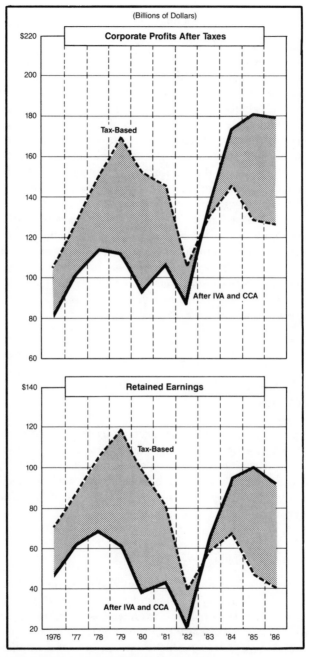

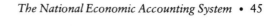

Sources: U.S. Department of Commerce; The Conference Board.

Figure 2–17. Adjustments to Corporate Profits (after Taxes) and Retained Earnings

Property Incomes and Wage Incomes

The national accounts identify a figure for compensation of employees, including supplements to wages and salaries, or *fringes*. They also identify a corporate-earnings figure, the dividend component of which is a part of personal income. In addition, the accounts identify two other property incomes—the rental income earned by persons (a later section deals with the origin of most individual rental incomes) and an interest income. In the total national income, the interest figure represents the excess of interest payments made by the business sector over the interest payments received by the business sector. The figure is thus the net return of owners of capital on their lending to the business sector, just as the dividends are the paid-out return on the equity investment in the business sector.

For purposes of longer-term analysis, comparisons are often drawn between the compensation of employees, as **labor income,** and the total of dividends, interest, and rental incomes, as **property income** (see figure 2–18). The comparison is usable, although perhaps too much can be made of it. There is no clearly defined *labor class* or *property class* in the United States; the vast majority of households receive both kinds of income (particularly since home ownership involves a rental income).

Relations between the Output and Income Sides of the Accounts

The national accounts describe an accounting entity that produces output and income, and then proceeds to use the income to consume virtually all of its own output. Relating components of the output side of the system to the income side produces some of the most useful analysis available in the national accounts. It also produces some accounting complexities that are not present in normal business accounting.

Personal Income, Spending, and Saving

The components of the national accounts that bear on the behavior of the personal sector produce by-products that are of great significance to all business, but particularly to the consumer-goods industries and retailers, whose activities represent nearly two-thirds of the total economy.

If personal income is reduced by the tax burden of individuals levied against them by all governments, the resulting figure is the famous **disposable personal income**—that is, income available after taxes. If the *spending* of individuals is subtracted from this figure, and if we also remove the interest payments of individuals (excluding payments on residential mortgage interest)

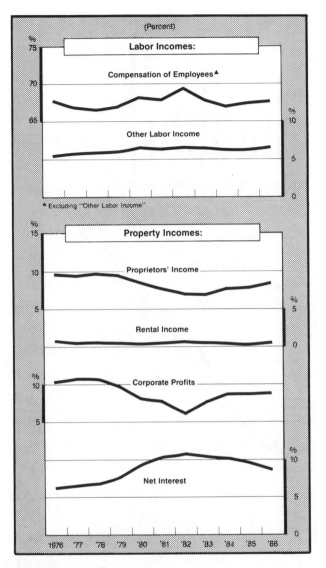

▲ Excluding "Other Labor Income."

Sources: U.S. Department of Commerce; The Conference Board.

Figure 2–18. Labor Incomes and Property Incomes as a Percentage of National Income

and certain transfers from the individual sector to other sectors of the accounts (for example, the transfer of funds to relatives abroad), the resulting figure—now only a small fraction of the personal income with which this sector of the accounts begins—is, conceptually, **personal saving** (see figure 2–19).

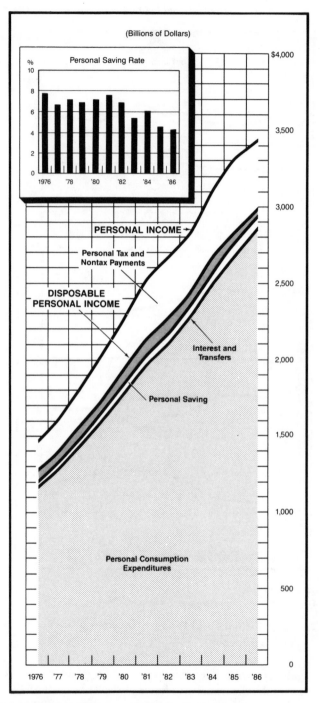

(Billions of Dollars)

Personal Saving Rate

PERSONAL INCOME →

Personal Tax and
Nontax Payments

DISPOSABLE
PERSONAL INCOME

Interest and
Transfers

Personal Saving

Personal Consumption
Expenditures

Sources: U.S. Department of Commerce; The Conference Board.

Figure 2–19. Personal Income, Spending, and Saving

This saving figure, available quarterly in the national accounts both as a dollar amount and as a percentage of disposable income, is widely, if a little uneasily, regarded as a measure of the saving propensity of the U.S. consumer and of the U.S. personal sector as a whole. The percentage figure historically has run at 5 to 6 percent of income, but it has recently been erratic and abnormally low. As might be expected, the figure tends to rise in any quarter in which a tax reduction suddenly becomes effective, as it did in the third quarters of 1981, 1982, and 1983. Thereafter, it appears to settle gradually back again as the increase in disposable income resulting from a tax reduction gradually finds its way into the spending stream.

Other important cautions about the personal-saving figure are in order. In the first place, it is statistically very volatile because it is measured as a lumpy, undifferentiated aggregate—simply the subtraction of one very large number (personal consumption expenditures) from another very large number (disposable personal income). Even small percentage errors in the measurement of one or both of these large aggregates produce disproportionately large errors in the personal saving rate. In addition, the saving rate shares with the rest of the national accounts the exclusion of all income flows resulting from capital gains and losses; there have been years in which these gains and losses (predominantly in the changing value of financial assets) have had a dramatic impact on the financial condition of the personal sector. The saving rate misses all the accumulated capital gains in holdings of residential real estate.

Finally, the saving concept here is so broad that it is difficult to interpret. Because of the conceptual structure of the two aggregates whose difference it represents, the saving figure is enormously inclusive. It covers all net saving in financial forms (increases in net new saving, but not capital gains on existing holdings), as well as saving in physical forms (net acquisition of equity in residential property), as well as net increase in the cash value of insurance reserves (in general, the premium payments, less expenses of the insurance companies—including their profits if they are not mutual companies). It includes all increases in pension reserves, and it reflects the activities of unincorporated businesses (discussed later). Other figures, outside the framework of the national accounts, can be used to resolve this gross aggregate into its components—particularly the resolution into *financial saving* less increase in financial liabilities, and *saving in tangible assets* less the applicable depreciation.

Despite the awkwardness of the measure, it is widely used, particularly in international comparisons. The figure is often said to indicate that the U.S. personal saving rate is strikingly low relative to the prevailing rates in many other countries—most strikingly West Germany and Japan. The implication is that the United States, in its present stage, is a high-consumption, low-saving society (see figure 2–20), a condition whose origin and present importance were described in chapter 1.

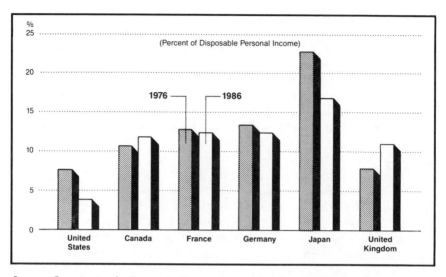

Sources: Organization for Economic Cooperation and Development; The Conference Board.

Figure 2–20. International Comparisons of Personal Saving Rates

Unincorporated Business in the National Accounts

For some obvious reasons, it is difficult to deal with the huge and diversified **unincorporated business** sector in the national accounts. A corporation is an accounting entity. The accounting shield around it identifies its income as a corporate income (not the income of the shareholders who own the corporation), and it is treated as a taxable entity by the federal tax structure. The unincorporated business, on the other hand, has neither an accounting nor a legal shield protecting its income and assets. It is obvious enough that the income drawn from an unincorporated business by its owner is personal income to the owner—as are, of course, the wage and salary payments to employees of unincorporated business. But what can be done about changes in the net worth of the unincorporated enterprise?

On the income side, the national accounts do not segregate unincorporated business from the personal sector. Personal income thus includes all proprietors' income, plus the increase in the net worth of the unincorporated enterprise. Since the increase in net worth is not expended on consumer goods, all of this element of personal income moves into the measure of saving. The somewhat strange result is that personal saving reflects increases in the capital assets (after depreciation) and inventories of unincorporated enterprises.

On the expenditure side, the *purchases* of unincorporated enterprises appear in the gross national product account in the appropriate categories;

that is, their purchases of all business equipment appear in the nonresidential-construction and producer-durables categories, and the change in their inventory position is a component of the change in business inventories. The treatment of unincorporated business in the accounts thus straddles the personal sector and the business sector; the income side is in the personal sector, the expenditures in the business sector. Only a great deal of processing can reveal the relations among income, spending, and saving for these businesses; in any event, the issue rarely arises in general analysis and forecasting.

Aggregate Business Income and Investment

On the output side of the national accounts, the purchases of all business (corporate and unincorporated) consist of all the components of gross private domestic investment—the outlays for plant and equipment by all business and outlays for net additions to inventory (a net reduction of inventory is a negative entry, a partial disinvestment). All residential construction is also a business outlay, even though it may end up in the household sector (discussed later in this chapter).

The definition of **business gross income** in the national accounts, applicable to this concept of business expenditure, is necessarily somewhat fuzzy and complicated. It includes the retained earnings of the corporate sector (the dividend payments are properly allocated to personal income). But in accordance with the requirement that all capital gains and losses be removed from the accounts, the retained earnings are reduced by the amount of inventory profit included in the reported earnings. Similarly, the retained earnings so calculated are then adjusted for any overdepreciation or underdepreciation charged in the corporate sector (the so-called capital consumption adjustment), which represents the difference between the depreciation charged in tax-based accounting and the true exhaustion of capital, as estimated by the U.S. Department of Commerce. Corporations are now overdepreciating on a tax basis, as a consequence of the liberalization of depreciation in the 1981 legislation. (More recent legislation has modified the effects, but not removed them.) The ordinary calculation of retained earnings in 1986 was reduced accordingly to remove the inventory profit, and then increased to offset the overdepreciation of capital.

To this adjusted retained-earnings figure is added the actual aggregate depreciation of the corporate sector, to yield the corporate cash flow after taxes and dividends. (Remember, these accounts are *gross*. The output side is not reduced for exhaustion of capital; hence the income side must incorporate the depreciation flow.)

Finally, a **depreciation allowance** for all noncorporate business must be added to business gross income. This figure includes all depreciation of capital facilities owned by unincorporated business, including farms. Since home ownership is treated as a business in the national accounts (that is why residential building is treated as an investment component), a depreciation flow against all residential building facilities is also included in the business cash flow.

That is the business sector in the national accounts. Though not conceptually beautiful, it is the best that can be done given two factors: the difficulty in treating unincorporated business as having one foot in the personal sector and one foot in the business sector; and the need to treat home ownership as a business activity.

The results are nevertheless coherent. As would be expected, the business sector is the characteristic investing sector for the system as a whole. The personal sector saves, on balance; the business sector invests, on balance. Figure 2–21 shows the expenditure of the business sector and its income; the characteristic gap is net business expenditure, or net investment of the business sector.

Housing in the National Accounts

The treatment of **home ownership** in the national accounts illustrates the kinds of special problems that distinguish national accounting from conventional business accounting. In the national accounts, it would be unfortunate if a simple change in the legal status of an occupied dwelling—that is, from a rent status to an ownership status—should affect the gross national product, since no real change in any measurable output occurs. In order to avoid such a change, the national accounts accept the rental cost of a rented property as a dollar measure of the housing service the property provides. For owner-occupied dwellings, the accounts estimate the rental value of an owner-occupied dwelling and all the costs associated with owning the dwelling.

In effect, the homeowner is in the business of owning a dwelling unit and renting it to himself. The *imputed* or estimated rental value is the owner's expenditure, included in personal-consumption expenditures for services. The income from ownership of the property, included under rental income in personal income, is the rental value (which is consumed in kind) minus the costs, which include real estate taxes, property insurance, depreciation, and interest on the residential mortgage (if any). In recent years the imputed rental value of owner-occupied dwellings has exceeded $250 billion, and the associated costs have exceeded $200 billion (see figure 2–22). It is an odd arrangement, which generates an income flow, an expenditure, and a profit from being in the home-owning business; but it is necessary to assure parallel treatment for owner-occupied and renter-occupied dwellings.

One consequence is that the output side of the accounts includes both the value of ongoing construction work in building new residential facilities, and the occupancy values provided by the existing stock of residential facilities

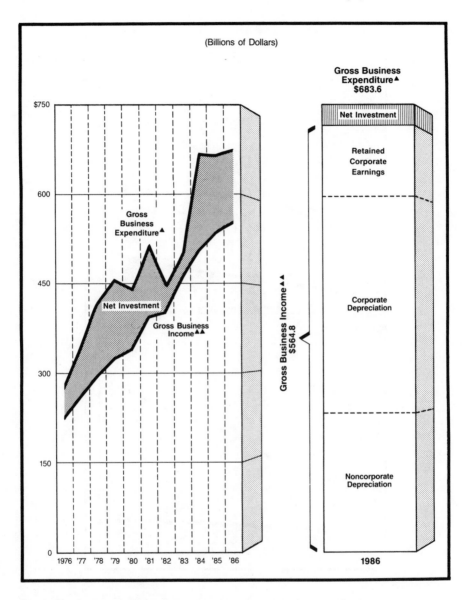

▲ Gross Private Domestic Investment.

▲▲ Retained Corporate Earnings plus Corporate and Noncorporate Depreciation (or Gross Private Saving less Personal Saving).

Sources: U.S. Department of Commerce; The Conference Board.

Figure 2–21. Business Income and Investment

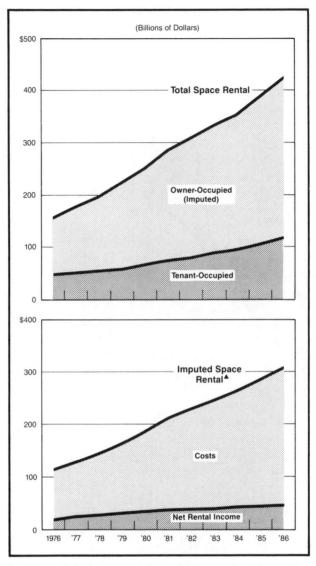

▲ Owner-occupied.
Sources: U.S. Department of Commerce; The Conference Board.

Figure 2–22. Housing in the National Accounts

(whether rented or owned). Transfers of homes through purchase and sale do not, of course, represent a form of output and are not included in the gross national product; and the capital gains from appreciation of residential real estate are excluded from all the accounts, as are all other forms of capital gains and losses.

Saving and Investment in the National Accounts

The terms **saving and investment** have special significance in the national accounts. Their definitions, and the relationship between them, develop inevitably out of the accounting system; but they turn out to be extremely useful in tracing the history of the business cycle, in understanding its causes, and in forecasting its future course.

It will be recalled that for the system as a whole, total output, total expenditure, and total income are equal quantities. If certain expenditures are designated *consumption* and the remainder are designated *investment,* then it follows that saving equals total income minus consumption, and investment is total output minus consumption. *Given the equality of income and output, it follows that saving equals investment, no matter how consumption is defined.*

The accounts, in fact, define consumption as consisting of all personal spending, even including such consumer-durables categories as automobiles, appliances, home furnishings, and other durable goods; and all outlays of government, whether they are for durable goods, construction, payroll, or crop inventory. The investment side of this definition includes all business expenditures — for housing, nonresidential construction, producer durables, and net change in inventory — in other words, gross private domestic investment. Also included as investment are net exports; when net exports are negative (that is, when the United States is running an import surplus) this becomes a negative entry on the investment side of the system, or disinvestment.

The saving flows that equal the investment flows consist of the personal saving done in the personal sector, the retained earnings and depreciation of the business sector (including depreciation flows on homes), and the surplus of the government sector (a government deficit is *negative* saving, or dissaving). The depreciation flows need to be included, since these are gross accounts, seeking a gross saving estimate. Table 2–4 shows the identity of the two sides of the account, with a minor statistical discrepancy.

For the total system, then, saving and investment are almost interchangeable terms; they are an accounting identity. *For any accounting period, aggregate saving will equal aggregate investment.*

However, just as the identity of sources and uses of funds in a corporate statement applies only to the total business entity and not to its divisions or subsidiaries, so in the national accounts the saving-investment identity prevails for the entire economy, but not for the individual sectors. Only when the sectors are added together is the identity achieved.

The personal sector is generally a large net saver; its income exceeds its outlay, and the balance is referred to as a net personal saving. The business sector is characteristically a net investor; that is, it spends more on construction, machinery, and inventories than its gross cash flow from earnings and depreciation. The government sector may be a saver (when it runs a surplus)

Table 2–4
Gross Saving
(billions of dollars)

	1976	1986
1. GROSS SAVING	**$283.0**	**$532.0**
2. GROSS PRIVATE SAVING	**321.4**	**679.8**
3.　Personal saving	95.8	130.6
4.　Undistributed corporate profits with inventory valuation and capital consumption adjustments ...	46.4	92.6
5.　　Undistributed profits	71.4	40.0
6.　　Inventory valuation adjustment...............	–14.9	6.5
7.　　Capital consumption adjustment	–10.1	46.0
8.　Corporate capital consumption allowances with capital consumption adjustment	107.5	282.8
9.　Noncorporate capital consumption allowances with capital consumption adjustment	71.7	173.8
10.　Wage accruals less disbursements	0.0	0.0
11. Government Surplus or Deficit (—), National Income and Product Accounts	**–38.4**	**–147.8**
12.　Federal	–53.5	–204.7
13.　State and local	15.2	56.8
14. Capital Grants Received by the United States (net)	**0.0**	**0.0**
15. GROSS INVESTMENT........................	**286.6**	**527.1**
16.　Gross private domestic investment	277.7	671.0
17.　Net foreign investment	9.0	–143.9
18. Statistical Discrepancy	**3.6**	**–4.9**

Sources: U.S. Department of Commerce; The Conference Board.

or a dissaver or investor, if its expenditures exceed its income. The international sector may be a net investor, when it is running a surplus, or a disinvestor (a saver) when it is running a deficit. The historical behavior of each of the sectors is shown in figure 2–23.

There is, of course, no reason at all why the intentions of savers and investors *at the beginning of an accounting period* should reflect such an identity. For example, if consumers are particularly confident of the future and have strong propensities to spend, they may wish to increase their spending and *save less*. At the same time, the business sector, perhaps encouraged by the same underlying conditions, may wish to *invest more*. Of this situation it is said that the ex ante (before-the-fact) intentions to save and invest are *not* in balance.

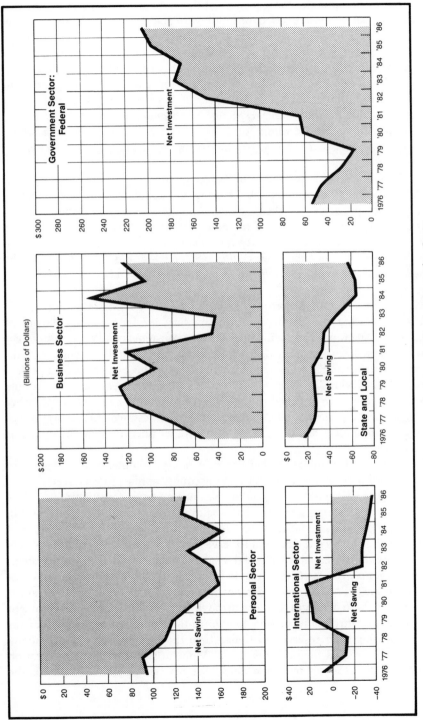

Figure 2–23. Saving and Investment, by Sectors

Let us examine the consequences of this imbalance, however. In the real world, consumers will in effect be bidding for such material resources as steel (which enters into automobiles and appliances) at the same time that the business sector is bidding for steel (for plant construction, machinery, and perhaps to build up inventories of steel); and steel production will accordingly rise. The same condition will prevail for a host of other goods and services, including labor itself. *An excess of investing intentions over saving intentions thus carries the suggestion of an expanding economy. Conversely, an excess of saving intentions over investing intentions connotes a falling economy—that is, a level of aggregate demand inadequate to support current production.*

In response to these forces, the resulting movement of the economy itself eliminates the ex ante imbalance. During an expansion, consumer incomes rise, tending to elevate their saving, and government revenues rise (as taxable incomes rise), tending to reduce its deficit (dissaving); the reverse happens in a recession. *When we look back on any accounting period, the ex ante differences have been obliterated in these and other ways by the behavior of the economy itself.* An ex post—after-the-fact—identity has been restored.

In forecasting, it is useful to know where the ex ante intentions stand. The forecasting profession, accordingly, has developed a large array of surveys of spending and saving intentions of consumers and businesses to get at precisely that issue. A budget projection by the federal government, indicating whether and in what degree it will run a surplus or a deficit, is a projection of the saving (or dissaving) intentions of government, which accounts for the significance attached to the budget projections by forecasters. Other things being equal, a budget deficit, being an investment (dissaving) intention, is stimulative to the business system; a surplus (a saving intention) is restrictive.

A last, unfortunately rather abstruse, note is required. The identity of saving and investment in the national accounts applies to real saving—real in the sense of a withholding of current income from consumption. It does not reflect the increases in financial wealth that may result from increases in the value of existing and tangible assets. And it does not reflect *creation* of new credit, of which the Federal Reserve and the commercial banking system are continuously capable. The value of the financial assets in the system, therefore, may rise faster than would be indicated by the real saving out of income. If the Federal Reserve *monetizes* the federal debt—that is, if it arranges to lend to the federal government through its own purchases of government securities, or through its powers to enlarge the lending of commercial banks by increasing their reserve positions—then the real saving is being supplemented by created financial resources. Monetarists stress that this creation of financial resources over and above the real saving of the system is the ultimate source of inflation. According to this reasoning, it is not the budget deficit itself that is inflationary; it is the creation of financial wealth over and above the real saving rate, as the Federal Reserve contributes to the financing of the deficit, that is the true cause of inflation because it violates the ex post identity of saving and investment. In this respect, as in many others, the real world departs from the conceptual world of the national accounts. Forecasters accordingly pay a great deal of attention to the political and economic forces that operate on the federal budget, and on the Federal Reserve's behavior with respect to the creation of money and credit (see chapter 5).

The Federal Government in the National Accounts

Within the conceptual framework of the national accounts there is an accounting of **federal government receipts, expenditures,** and **surplus or deficit** that very largely mirrors the actual budget of the federal government as legislated by the Congress and experienced by the U.S. Treasury. The conceptual differences between the two sets of accounts are not really substantial; there are some differences in timing (that is, some accounts are picked up on an accrual basis rather than the cash basis used in the federal budget) and minor differences in coverage. On the whole, what happens to the budget legislated by the Congress is accurately reflected in the federal-government sector of the national accounts. The national accounts have a big advantage, however; the federal sector's operations are available quarterly, at seasonally adjusted annual rates, and they can be compiled into calendar-year annual data comparable to the data available for all the other sectors. (The legislated budget is on a September 30 fiscal year.) The national-accounts version of the federal budget is a preferred statistical device for integrating the federal government's operations into a forecast.

As reflected in the national accounts, the receipts of the federal government include all personal tax receipts, corporate-profits tax accruals, and indirect business tax receipts—excise taxes and customs duties. They also include receipts of the social-insurance funds. Expenditures include all purchases of goods and services, and all transfer payments, as well as grants-in-aid to state and local governments, the net interest paid (interest paid minus interest receipts), and the net subsidies of the federal government to government enterprises (subsidies less the current surpluses of government enterprises). If the expenditures are subtracted from the receipts, the resulting surplus or deficit closely parallels the budget operations recorded in the government's actual balance of receipts and expenditures on an *annual* basis; but quarterly comparisons are complicated by the immense seasonal patterns

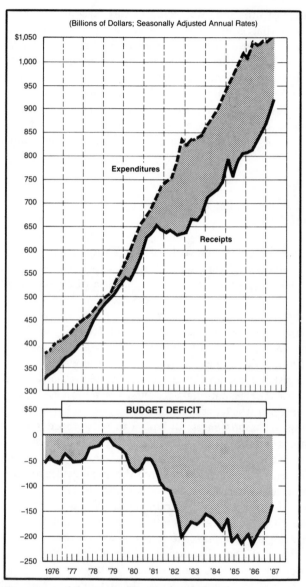

(Billions of Dollars; Seasonally Adjusted Annual Rates)

Sources: U.S. Department of Commerce; The Conference Board.

Figure 2–24. The Federal Budget in the National Accounts

in budget receipts, which are not available on a seasonally adjusted basis. The national-income version of the federal budget appears in figure 2–24. Forecasts of the national accounts thus generally produce usable forecasts, or at least insights, concerning the future budget position of the federal government implied by the general business forecast, and hence some insight into the policy issues ahead.

Long-Term Trends in the National Accounts

The statistical record of the GNP goes back almost four decades with nearly perfect conceptual consistency; with only modest conceptual change, the series goes back to 1929. (Even earlier data, but with considerable conceptual inconsistency, go back to the turn of the century.) The long-term record of the accounts makes only a minor direct contribution to short-term forecasting; but longer-term projections of where the economy will be, ten years or even only five years in the future, properly draw on the long historical record as the basis for calculating normal or expectable growth. These long-term projections are an attempt to ignore the business cycle; that is, they deal with a period in which recessions and expansions might be expected to cancel out, revealing long-term movements dominated by underlying conditions of growth rather than of a cyclical nature.

Since price forecasting is uncertain and difficult even over the long term, projections of the national economy that run beyond the ordinary forecasting concerns of the business cycle tend to deal with the real (inflation-adjusted) GNP as the available reality. Figure 2–25 shows the long-term progress of the GNP expressed in 1982 prices—that is, with all the output in all the years valued at 1982 value per unit, thus removing the price effects. Simple logarithmic (constant percentage) growth rates are fitted in the chart to the entire span since 1947, and then to subparts of the historical record; and the growth rates associated with all these periods are indicated on the growth lines. Beneath this chart for the aggregate appear lines representing the growth trends of the major components of GNP; these are calculated for a variety of major markets for the period 1976–1986. At least for these broad aggregates, the chart reveals the relatively fast-growing and relatively slow-growing components of the GNP; but within these subaggregates there is a vast, tumultuous shift of products and markets away from slow-growing or dying markets and to rapidly accelerating, newer markets. Still further disaggregation of these subtotals is possible, of course, and is typically engaged in by individual companies seeking to understand the future of their present composition of output, and seeking guidance on the more vigorous markets available to them.

As illustration of other uses for the long-term accounts, figure 2–26 compares the U.S. growth rate, in terms of inflation-adjusted GNP, with the growth rates being experienced by the more important of our Western trading partners, as calculated from their own, generally comparable, data.

Figure 2–27 depicts U.S. growth rates in the broadest possible segregation of the accounts—into output of goods, services, and construction. The

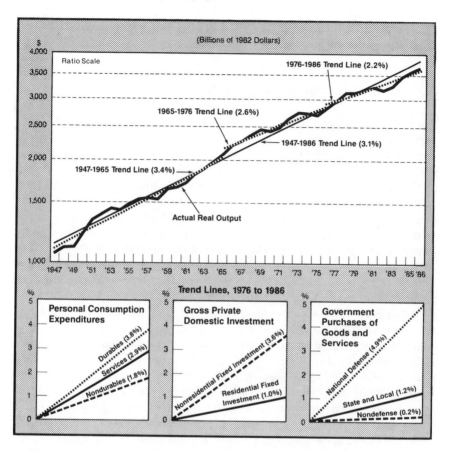

Sources: U.S. Department of Commerce; The Conference Board.

Figure 2–25. Long-Term Trends in Output

chart bears out the often-expressed judgment that the United States has become increasingly a service-producing economy. However, the chart carries the suggestion that the markets for goods are by no means approaching exhaustion in the United States; it may even suggest that in coming decades, the production of goods may be sustained at least as well as the production of services.

Actual and Middle-Expansion Trend Output

A recent extension of national accounting seeks to describe the course of our real *potential* for producing the GNP—that is, the resources of capital facil-

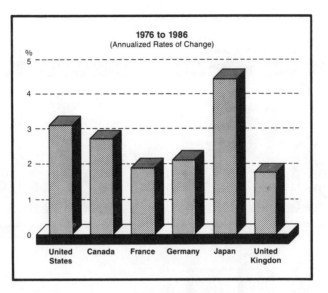

Sources: International Monetary Fund; The Conference Board.

Figure 2–26. GNP Growth, Here and Abroad

ities and manpower that are the real inputs. The **middle-expansion,** or **cyc-lically adjusted,** trend of **output** (formerly called the *high-employment* GNP) shown in figure 2–28 is a description of our supposed economic potential. Charted with it is our actual output—the degree to which we have achieved the potential; the gap between the two lines charted, also shown as a per-centage of our potential, represents our shortfall from the potential. There is no single, ordained high-employment GNP; rather, several versions of it are calculated (by the U.S. Department of Commerce and others). The differ-ences among such series will reflect differences in judgment about what unemployment rate should be associated with the concept of *high employ-ment,* as well as what kind of productivity gain should be assumed in the high-employment trajectory of output.

It is generally accepted that as the system's output falls away from its high-employment potential, the resources thus made idle compete with the resources in use and tend to arrest inflation. Conversely, as actual output begins to approach the potential closely, the idle resources shrink, competi-tion for supply increases, and the inflation rate tends to rise. These proposi-tions are often related to conventional business-cycle propostions about infla-tion, that is, an accelerating business recovery would normally strengthen prices, whereas recession would weaken them. In some periods—1983 is a good illustration—the two sets of reasoning about inflation tend to be off-

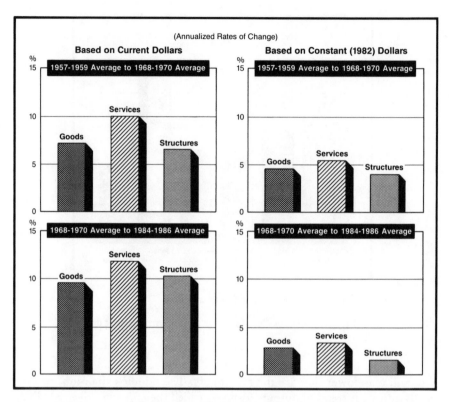

Sources: U.S. Department of Commerce; The Conference Board.

Figure 2–27. Growth Rates, by Type of Output

setting; a very vigorous recovery with implicit price consequences occurred at a time when the economy was still experiencing a substantial shortfall from high employment.

These considerations were clearly reflected in discussions of inflation prospects in 1984: powerfully growing markets, but still abundantly available supply. Since 1984, the growth of markets has slowed, and a much larger share of demand in the United States has been served by imports; that is, U.S. markets for goods have grown more rapidly than U.S. production of goods. These propositions, drawn from the national accounts, provide a useful way of looking at the complicated problems faced by the Federal Reserve—whether or not to restrain a vigorous recovery for fear of inflation,

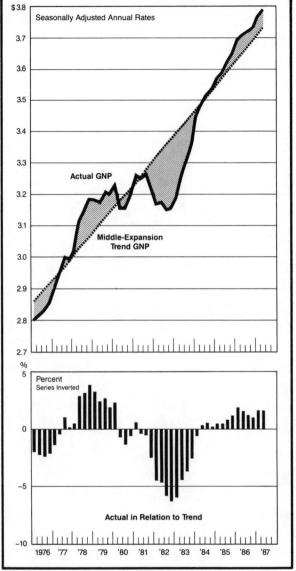

(Trillions of 1982 Dollars)

Seasonally Adjusted Annual Rates

Actual GNP

Middle-Expansion
Trend GNP

Percent
Series Inverted

Actual in Relation to Trend

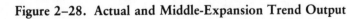

Sources: U.S. Department of Commerce; The Conference Board.

Figure 2–28. Actual and Middle-Expansion Trend Output

even while the volume of idle resources remains substantial. In these and manifold other uses, the national accounts continue to play a central role in debates about the state of business, and the suitability of existing or proposed policies of the federal government.

3
The Data Stream

S tanding behind the national accounts, and contributing the raw materials from which the national accounts are produced, is a nearly infinite stream of data—almost all of it issued monthly, and almost all of it reported with interest in the business press. These are the figures that make the short-term news; they give business journalism its raw materials and its daily excitement. Any inclusive compilation of this Niagara of data would make a formidable reference work; indeed, the U.S. Department of Commerce publishes biennially an oversized two-hundred-page volume of such data that is itself incomplete, even though it goes far beyond the needs of a sophisticated observer intent on watching major developments in the U.S. business system.

What follows here is a highly selective collection of the principal indicators that make the news and that nudge economic opinion in one direction or another. The statistics described here are organized by sector. A ruthless selection process has driven the number of series (and even the number of sectors) down to what we can all hope to grasp and retain, so that when the next release in the series is reported in the business press, it will be recognized and understood for what it is. Series whose principal bearing is on the behavior of the business cycle, or on the functioning of economic policy, are reserved for a later chapter. Here we are after the raw materials of economic appraisal—the staccato reporting of a small number of very important figures that shed their light each time they appear, and then disappear from the news until their next release a month later. Typical monthly and quarterly calendars of statistical releases, showing their approximate date of release and the compiling source, appear in the appendixes.

The Personal Sector: Income, Spending, Credit Use

The personal sector buys about two-thirds of total national output—easily the dominant component of U.S. business. About half of all the personal spending is for *services,* a varied and elusive outlay that runs all the way from rents to haircuts. Far more interesting, from a general analytic viewpoint, is the expenditure rate on goods at retail—a figure covered by a retail-sales release published by the U.S. Department of Commerce on about the thirteenth day of every month, covering all retail volume in the preceding month.

The **retail sales** figure is broken down into durable goods (those that presumably last three years or more) and nondurable goods (everything else, including food, clothing and shoes, gasoline and oil, and other miscellaneous soft goods). The principal interest attaches to the sales of durable goods, and most particularly of motor vehicles and parts, which account for about half of all durable goods.

Figure 3–1 shows the recent composition of aggregate retail volume. The monthly data are seasonally adjusted, but not adjusted for inflation. This is dollar volume at the nation's retail counters. The sales volume of automotive dealers (including the gross volume of used-car sales), of retail outlets for durable goods other than automobiles, and of several types of soft goods outlets are shown separately. General merchandise stores, which may sell durables as well as soft goods, are classified in soft goods; the classification is by type of store, not by type of merchandise. Each monthly release revises the figure for the preceding month; the revisions (based on more complete data) are often very large.

Among the important influences affecting the current and prospective volume of retail trade are the rate of growth of personal income (a component of the quarterly national accounts, but produced by the U.S. Department of Commerce monthly); the psychological attitudes of consumers; and the use of consumer credit, particularly to finance big-ticket durable goods.

The monthly figure on personal income is an inclusive measure of the flow of income to households, and is thus a major indicator of the probable trend of retail markets. It is a broad figure that moves smoothly over the short term; sharp changes in retail spending occur even while the income flow maintains a steady trend.

Analysis of the surveys of **consumer attitudes** (done not by the government but by such private nonprofit institutions as the University of Michigan and The Conference Board) reveals no close short-term correspondence with current retail volume; but a prolonged rise or decline in sentiment, sustained over several months, has large and obvious significance. Some of the surveys of consumer attitudes also report on the buying plans of consumers. These series are highly volatile and have little short-term application (see figure 3–2).

The statistics on use of **consumer credit** are compiled by the Federal Reserve and are issued about thirty days after the month to which they apply. They include estimates of the total amount of credit outstanding, by type— installment credit for automobiles and other durables purchases, and per-

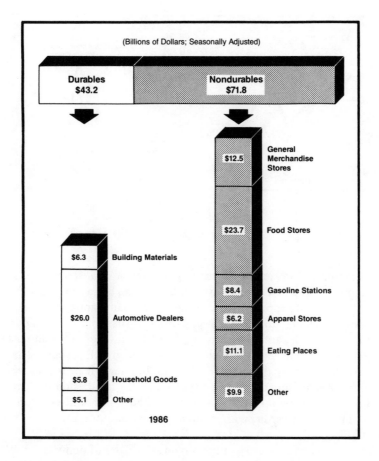

(Billions of Dollars; Seasonally Adjusted)

Durables $43.2

Nondurables $71.8

General Merchandise Stores $12.5

Food Stores $23.7

Building Materials $6.3

Gasoline Stations $8.4

Automotive Dealers $26.0

Apparel Stores $6.2

Eating Places $11.1

Household Goods $5.8

Other $9.9

Other $5.1

1986

Sources: U.S. Department of Commerce; The Conference Board.

Figure 3–1. The Composition of Retail Volume

sonal (unsecured) loans. This is *short-term* credit; mortgage credit is not included. In addition to the amount outstanding, the releases used to include measures of the rate of *new* credit extension and repayment, but these very useful series were abandoned in one of the budget crises that periodically beset the statistical agencies in Washington. Credit use by consumers seems to be a violent cyclical accompaniment to retail trade; its volume, in terms of net increase in debt outstanding, oscillates dramatically with general business conditions and parallels the behavior of the automobile market, to which much of installment credit is directed.

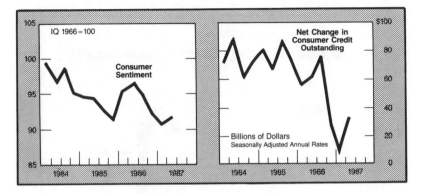

Sources: University of Michigan; Federal Reserve; The Conference Board.

Figure 3–2. Consumer Attitudes and the Use of Credit

Beginning in 1987, the deductibility of interest on installment credit has entered on a swift phase-out. Consumer borrowing has accordingly shifted to debt on residential property—the "home equity loan," apparently beloved by borrower and lender alike. Interest payments on such loans are relatively low and fully deductible; and there is more than $1 trillion of as yet unmortgaged equity available. The sudden birth and awesome growth of such debt is not yet the subject of a separate statistical series, but never fear, it will be. It may be worth remembering that 30 percent of all U.S. families do not own their own homes and have no equity to mortgage. Such lost souls are still dependent on installment credit, with its higher rates, shorter terms, and declining deductibility.

The automobile industry releases figures on sales of domestic models for periods covering ten days of sale—that is, three times a month (the figures are seasonally adjusted by the U.S. Department of Commerce, as well as by private agencies). The production rate for the domestic automobile industry is reported every month in "Ward's Automotive Reports," an industry trade publication, along with figures on dealer inventories, and the prices of used cars. An automobile purchase shows the U.S. consumer in his most revealing moment; automobile sales are thus a dominant (but highly variable) influence on impressions of the strength or weakness of retail sales. A strong automobile trend is seldom contradicted by the rest of the retail market.

The Housing Market

Housing construction and sale is a deceptively small component of the total system; residential-construction activity accounts for only about 4 percent of total national output. It is a highly volatile industry, however, and the violent waves—business cycles—in the housing industry are transmitted down the line to such major industries as forest products, nonferrous metals, and fabricated construction materials and supplies.

The basic statistic on activity in the housing industry, as shown in figure 3–3, relates to **housing units started;** the release is called "Housing Starts" and is published by the U.S. Department of Commerce in the middle of each month, covering activity in the preceding month. A *housing start* refers to the breaking of ground—the actual commencement of construction. The starts figures are available for single-family dwellings and for multiple (apartment-house) structures (each apartment of which is considered a start). In addition to starts, the Commerce Department also collects the rate of building-permit issuance, a figure that is assumed to lead starts by a month or more. Figures are also available, from the same source, on units completed (with an average lag from start to completion of about three months), and on both new and existing homes sold and for sale.

The housing market is, by its nature, a collection of regional markets. The U.S. Department of Commerce accordingly publishes considerable regional detail for its aggregate statistics; regional disparities in the total rate are common. Nevertheless, major movements in the aggregate industry, usually reflecting broad changes in economic conditions and the supply and price of mortgage credit, are generally reflected across the nation.

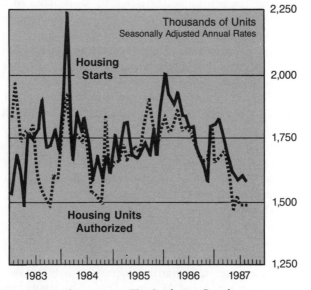

Sources: U.S. Department of Commerce; The Conference Board.

Figure 3–3. The Housing Industry: Starts and Building Permits

The housing market takes much of its striking volatility from its dependence on mortgage credit, and from the fluctuations, sometimes mountainous, in the interest rates available to mortgage borrowers. When money gets tight (for a description of this condition, see chapter 5 on economic policy), interest rates rise and potential buyers face increasingly unattractive carrying charges. The behavior of the housing market, as measured by the starts rate, is thus a kind of delayed mirror image of the behavior of mortgage interest rates, as shown in figure 3–3.

Some of the reasons for violent oscillations in the housing market in the past appear to be on their way to removal; builders in the housing industry are now larger, on average, and better established and financed. Deregulation has freed the thrift institutions that provide much of the mortgage money to compete for funds in the general capital market. The usury limitations on interest rates have been very largely removed, so that the scarcity of funds directly attributable to unworkable legal limitations on mortgage interest rates has almost disappeared. The fact remains, however: Very high interest rates inevitably discourage home buyers and depress the rate of housing starts.

Capital Spending and Its Sources

New investment by the private sector is widely considered to be a crucial component of the system's aggregate demand; private investment is the source of future growth and future increases in efficiency, on which improving living standards ultimately rest. **Capital outlay by business** constitutes, on average, about 13 percent of total demand, but its importance in the business cycle is far greater than the percentage would indicate. Spending by business for investment goods is the classical case of the economist's multiplier effect: A dollar of wages generated in the capital-goods industry will go to market in search of a consumer good, which will contribute to the production of another consumer good; wages paid in the course of the production of the second consumer good will seek a third, and so on. (The process attenuates because at each stage a portion of the generated income is saved, rather than spent.) It is generally estimated that a dollar of output in the machinery industries is worth something like three dollars of total GNP. The calculation may be a little loose, but the principle is sound enough. In its ascending phase, investment in plant and equipment is very stimulative to the total system; in its declining phase, it is very constrictive.

Given its importance, it is hardly surprising that the rate of capital spending is the subject of a large data industry, all by itself. In the national accounts, the industry is represented by nonresidential fixed investment, subdivided in turn into nonresidential construction and producer durables—plain old machinery and equipment (including automobiles bought by the

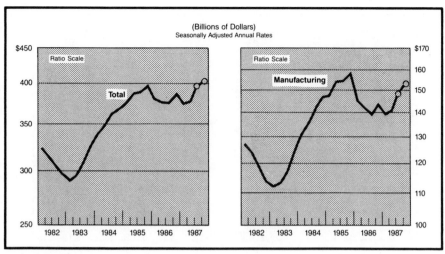

▲ Anticipated
Sources: U.S. Department of Commerce; The Conference Board.

Figure 3–4. The Trend of Capital Outlay

business sector). The U.S. Department of Commerce also produces a quarterly series on business expenditures for plant and equipment, which includes a past record, as well as a measure of anticipated outlays running two calendar quarters into the future. These are the basic data on expected plant and equipment outlay; they play a large role, for obvious reasons, in economic forecasting (see figure 3–4).

The business expenditures series differs from the all-inclusive series in the national accounts in that it excludes agricultural investment, as well as those smaller outlays (such as hand tools) that are normally expensed rather than depreciated. It provides running detail and six-month projections for manufacturing industries, and also for mining and service industries, including a broad category of commercial construction.

Behind this basic quarterly series lies a wealth of monthly data on the industry. Activity in the nonresidential construction industry, an important part of capital investment, is available monthly, about three weeks after the end of the month, from the U.S. Department of Commerce. It is broken down into a large number of categories: office buildings, industrial structures, shopping centers, and so on. Activity on the machinery side of capital outlay is described in the detailed breakdown of the industrial production index and in the general data on manufacturing industries (discussed later). The machine-tool industry, a small but volatile and significant part of the total, is reported on monthly by the National Machine Tool Builders Association.

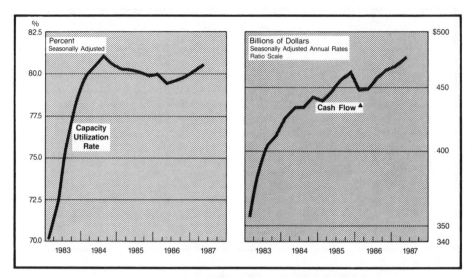

▲ Profits after tax plus charged depreciation (including over-depreciation).
Sources: Federal Reserve; U.S. Department of Commerce; The Conference Board.

Figure 3–5. Two Determinants of Capital Outlay

The Federal Reserve bravely attempts to estimate the **usage rate of capacity** in the U.S. system—bravely, because not much is known about abandonment rates, technological changes in the production functions of individual industries, or changing industry practices with respect to number of shifts. Nevertheless, it is widely assumed that these utilization figures, released by the Federal Reserve about a day after it releases its industrial production index (see below), have substantial bearing on the future of capital outlay (see figure 3–5). It does not take an economist to realize that business will spend very little on incremental plant and equipment at times when it is using only a low percentage of its existing capacity, and that its interest in capital outlay will rise as its current operating rates rise. It is generally assumed that operating rates around 85 percent of capacity would be associated with strong incentives to expand, and that these incentives are not present at 75 percent of capacity. Of course, about half of all capital outlay is for modernization, rather than for expansion (the distinction is powerfully difficult to draw in practice), so capital outlay goes on at all times—very vigorously, indeed, in situations where a new technology is displacing an older, more costly process.

The bulk of capital outlay is performed by corporations. The corporate cash flow, which constitutes a major source of funds for capital spending, is thus a further relevant element in appraising the outlook for capital outlay.

These figures are generated quarterly, within the national accounts, by adding retained earnings to the Commerce Department's measure of corporate depreciation allowances. In the early 1980s, tax-deductible depreciation costs (which constitute a cash flow to the corporation) rose sharply because of the accelerated-depreciation legislation of 1981. The rise in capital spending in 1983 and 1984 was accompanied by (and partly financed by) a surge in total cash flow (figure 3–5). Starting in 1987 (and even partly retroactively into 1986), tax reform has curtailed depreciation and dampened the rise in cash flow.

The Manufacturing Industries: Production, Sales, Inventories, Orders

The manufacturing sector of the U.S. economy constitutes only about 20 percent of the total, measured in terms of employment. However, although its share in the total has subsided and the share of services has grown, manufacturing activity remains in many respects the center of the system—a place where real wealth, as defined by anybody, is created. (There are large differences among economists on what constitutes real wealth.) Moreover, manufacturing, being a goods industry capable of experiencing fluctuations in desired levels of inventory holdings, has a special place in the business cycle. (There are, of course, no inventories of services output; services are consumed in the moment of their creation.) And because manufactured goods enter into international trade, the experience of manufacturing industries is heavily influenced by conditions affecting exports and imports.

Around the middle of each month, the Federal Reserve releases its monthly **industrial production index** for the preceding month. The index, among the most watched of all business statistics, measures industrial output (manufacturing, mining, and utilities) for the preceding month, calculating it as a percentage change from the base year of the series, which is still (unaccountably) all the way back in 1977. A mark of 130 for a month, in the industrial production index, signifies that output in that month, annualized, was 30 percent higher than in the base year. Although the relation to the base year is anachronistic, the month-to-month changes in the industrial production index are widely treated as representing the course of general industrial activity in the United States. Since the volatile, cyclical heavy-goods industries carry a disproportionate weight in the index, its behavior is more volatile than that of aggregate output. In general, a 6 percent annual growth rate of industrial output would suggest perhaps a 3 percent growth rate in *total* output (see figure 3–6).

The index is available in excruciating detail, all the way down to extremely small subindustries; it is therefore a source of close examination,

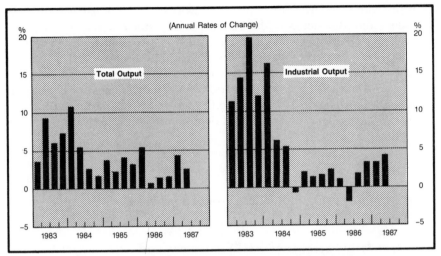

Sources: U.S. Department of Commerce; Federal Reserve; The Conference Board.

Figure 3–6. Real Growth Rates

not just by economists, but by sales and planning officers throughout industry as well.

The industrial production index is a measure of physical volume of output. Two weeks after it appears, the U.S. Department of Commerce issues an immense broadside of data on the dollar value of activity in manufacturing, including **sales, new orders, inventory holdings, and unfilled orders** (backlogs). The release itself carries substatistics for twenty major manufacturing industries—all seasonally adjusted, but with no adjustment for inflation. These are straight dollar figures, carrying all the significance and limitations that go with value figures. From the figures themselves, it is impossible to say how much of the change from a prior month results from price change, and how much from increased physical volume.

Within this immense structure of monthly data on manufacturing, particular interest attaches to the series on new orders, which presumably forecasts manufacturing activity in the future. The series on backlogs, or unfilled orders, helps to describe the direction of pressure on manufacturing activity (rising backlogs would seem to forecast higher production, and vice versa) and, most particularly, on the inventory condition of manufacturing.

Inventory conditions play a crucial role in the business cycle (see figure 3–7). Rapidly rising inventories must, in time, suggest that supply has achieved dominance over demand, and that at some future point production activity will begin to slow. Conversely, rapid liquidation of inventories (as occurred in the last half of 1982, for example) would appear to be unsustain-

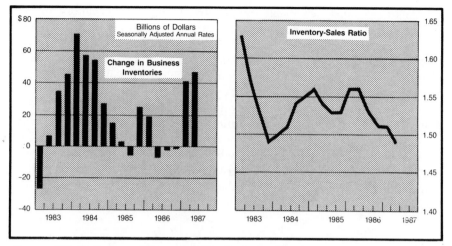

Sources: U.S. Department of Commerce; The Conference Board.

Figure 3–7. Two Ways of Looking at Inventories

able; the very effort to arrest liquidation of inventories would require rising orders and production.

The inventory figures produced within this amalgam of manufacturing data are supplemented in a release about ten days later that incorporates the inventories of wholesalers and retailers, producing an inventory figure for **total manufacturing and trade.** This series covers about 70 percent of all inventories in the system (excluded are agricultural inventories, inventories held by the construction industry, and inventories of nonmerchant wholesalers—wholesalers who do not take title).

This inventory concept differs from the inventory figure encountered in the national accounts, both because of these exclusions and because they are not corrected for whatever price appreciation (or depreciation) may have occurred in the existing stock of inventory. Since most of the manufacturing world is still on FIFO accounting, rising prices tend to increase the value of inventory even if there is no actual physical change. The manufacturing and trade inventory data do not correct for this discomfort, whereas the national accounting system, which must end up with a true measure of new production and nothing but new production, removes this so-called inventory profit from its measure of inventory demand. (The change in business inventories that appears as part of output in the national accounts can be maintained as a running total of inventory holdings. The resulting figure runs higher than the figure shown here for manufacturing and trade inventory by reason of the difference in coverage. The national-accounts figure is broader, but it is only available quarterly.)

Apart from this inescapable complexity, the aggregate inventory release (which lags about six weeks behind the fact) is an important monthly event for economists and the press. In late 1982 the release disclosed an enormous and unsustainable rate of inventory liquidation, and turned the outlook sharply upward. The figures showed immense inventory growth into the first three quarters of 1984, but sales had risen so sharply as to suggest that the expansion of inventory was entirely voluntary and no cause for alarm. This way of looking at inventory—as a ratio of inventory to the sales volume it must support, or, briefly, the inventory-sales ratio—offers a very useful second appraisal of the figures themselves, and is widely used in inventory analysis. So also is the relationship between unfilled orders and shipments, a calculation that produces a statistic called *months-of-backlog* at current ship-ment rates.

Employment and Unemployment

In the end, jobs, incomes and living standards are the ultimate criteria of the performance of an economic system. There are many other very important goals for a society as a whole—defense security, quality of life, fairness, personal liberty—but jobs, money, and material living standards are the central measures of pure economic performance. Not surprisingly, the U.S. statistical system generates an enormous volume of information, monthly, on labor-market conditions affecting U.S. workers.

Early every month, the Bureau of Labor Statistics produces the results of a massive sample survey of the employed and the unemployed. The defini-tions of unemployment make it very nearly a state of mind—that is, without a job and looking for work. The **employment and unemployment** figures, taken together, thus represent the U.S. **labor force,** which is now growing at a rate of about 2 million a year (see figure 3–8). When employment rises faster than that, as it did most decisively in 1983 and 1984, and again in much of 1987, unemployment shrinks; it is worth noting, however, that it takes job creation at an annual rate of 2 million simply to hold the number of unemployed constant. Unemployment is normally expressed as a percentage of the civilian labor force (see figure 3–9). Naturally, the percentage fluc-tuates dramatically in the course of the business cycle; it reached its postwar peak of almost 11 percent at the bottom of the 1982 recession, when almost 12 million Americans were out of work and looking for a job. (That's deep recession, but not depression; at the bottom of the Great Depression in the early 1930s, one in four Americans was out of work.)

Unemployment is a social statistic, as well as an economic statistic. The monthly census offers much material on who is unemployed (by age, sex, race) and the reasons for unemployment (lost a job, left a job, newly entered

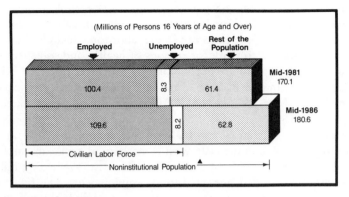

(Millions of Persons 16 Years of Age and Over)

▲ Excluding resident Armed Forces.
Sources: U.S. Department of Labor; The Conference Board.

Figure 3–8. Population and the Labor Force

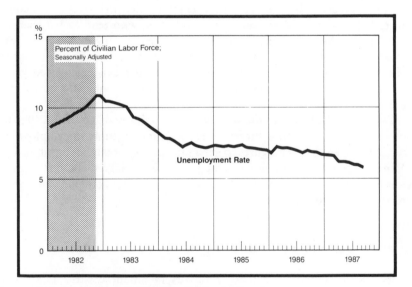

Sources: U.S. Department of Labor; The Conference Board.

Figure 3–9. The Cycle in the Unemployment Rate

into the labor force, or reentering the labor force). It is often argued (with some justice) that unemployment compensation tends to elevate unemployment, but it is worth noting that on average more than half the unemployed are unemployed because they lost a job.

In recent years, about 65 percent of the work-eligible population has been either working or looking for work. This figure is called the *labor force participation rate*. The one-third not in the labor force includes housewives, students, those unable to work for reasons of health, and so-called discouraged workers—those who are not looking for work because they believe no jobs are available. In part because of the rapid rise of female participation in the labor force, the percentage of all Americans actually at work rose to a new record in 1987.

The Census Bureau measures of labor force, employment, and unemployment are reported simultaneously with a measure of nonfarm employment produced by a large sample of actual payroll statistics, yielding figures on what is commonly called **nonagricultural employment.** The figures differ from the census results conceptually, in that they exclude the self-employed and also exclude agriculture; but they pick up the double employment of those working at two jobs. The nonagricultural employment figure is available in considerable industry detail for goods and services industries.

Changes in levels of employment are frequently accompanied by (and sometimes preceded by) changes in the length of the **work week.** This condition reflects the natural incentives of employers, who tend to lengthen the work week in the early stages of recovery, before engaging in the costly practice of hiring additional trainees. Conversely, as volume falls off, the work week tends to shrink before employers lay off their existing trained labor. The length of the work week thus becomes a leading indicator of business conditions.

Figures on the length of the work week are published in what is called the establishment basis payroll survey. Analysts often multiply the employment figures by the work-week figures to get a measure of total labor input into the system each month. Since labor is the predominant ingredient entering into economic activity, the monthly labor input measure is a good indicator of the direction of economic activity.

Prices, Wages, and Productivity

By its nature, economic activity proceeds in an inescapable mixture of physical characteristics and price characteristics. Every transaction in the market is ultimately valued in dollars; its trace in the statistical record reflects neither the physical units nor the price, but a compound of the two. Only in the narrowest of individual markets—say, the market for copper, or basic chemicals—is a physical unit of measure readily available. In the common case—for example, measuring the real output of the General Electric Company, or even of the steel industry—a dollar-value aggregate is the commonly available figure.

Changes in prices affect the whole stream of economic activity and stretch a veil—a so-called money illusion—across all the published data on sales, profits, and incomes of companies, industries, and the economy. The statistical system accordingly pays a great deal of attention to price information in order to develop price indexes by which money values can be deflated, to represent the underlying realities free from their price influence. The composition of such indexes—*index-number construction*—is a highly developed statistical specialty. For our purposes here, the thing to note is that a *price index* combines the prices of many items through a weighting system that reflects the *relative importance* of the items in a *base period,* for which a detailed array of expenditure patterns is available.

What is taken to be the major and most general price index for the U.S. economy is derived from the national accounts. The procedure for this deflation is described in chapter 2; the resulting index represents the U.S. price level, and changes in it are considered the general rate of inflation prevailing in the United States. The deflator is, of course, available for the individual components of the output side of the national accounts, yielding real rates of change in all the major demand sectors.

Behind this deflator and its various components lies an immense body of price data, organized into indexes that run from daily and weekly (for commodity prices) to substantial monthly indexes of prices for whole sectors of the system. The two principal monthly price indexes are the **consumer price index,** (the well-known CPI), which expresses prices at the retail level of goods and service prices, and the **producer price index** (the less famous PPI), which describes trends in the wholesale price level.

The consumer price index is an effort to represent in one number the price level (and the rate of inflation) confronting U.S. consumers (see figure 3–10). It covers services as well as goods; its weighting structure represents

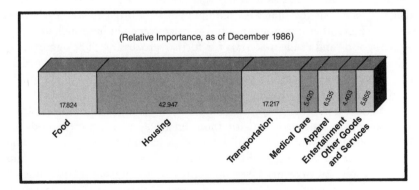

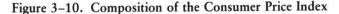

Sources: U.S. Department of Labor; The Conference Board.

Figure 3–10. Composition of the Consumer Price Index

the composition of outlay of urban consumers (the expenditure survey on which the weighting structure is based was done in 1982–1984). About 16 percent of the present index relates to food price, and 43 percent to housing, including the costs of renters and homeowners, and including fuels, household furnishings, and household operations. The weighting system of the index is a revelation of the importance of ongoing outlay to the consumer; new cars account for only 4.6 percent of the weight of the index. Major moves in the index, as in 1974, 1979, and 1987, usually reflect large gains in food, or housing costs, or both, but a spreading wave of price movement may well begin in a narrow but crucial sector, such as petroleum products.

Because it represents the price level confronting consumers, the CPI is frequently used to adjust personal incomes, converting them into their real purchasing power equivalents. The index is also widely used in labor negotiations, as an indication of the rate of price increase to which wage earners have been subject. It is embedded as a measure of the required cost-of-living adjustment (COLA) in union contracts, and in social security legislation itself. In such arrangements, the change in the index calls for an adjustment in an income flow; the income thus is said to be subject to *indexation*.

The release of a new monthly CPI, and the calculation of its change from the preceding month, always precipitates press comment on the general trend of inflation, not simply because it represents inflation itself, but because it is contractually linked to so many income flows. Extreme rises in the CPI thus have powerful offsetting effects; they deflate the existing income flow (they reduce its real-equivalent purchasing power) while at the same time evoking a growth of private wages and benefit incomes, contributing to a so-called wage-price (or price-wage) spiral.

The producer price index measures price developments at the wholesale price level of finished goods, underlying the retail level. Unlike the consumer price index, the PPI is concerned only with goods. The published PPI features finished goods, but the index is a component of a broader wholesale price index of which other components express price trends in intermediate (semi-finished) goods and crude materials for further processing. The aggregate of all three levels is called the *wholesale price index* (WPI). The intermediate index presumably forecasts future prices of finished goods, and the crude-materials index forecasts future prices of intermediate goods. In addition, the index provides a number of special groupings, including groupings for capital goods bought by business, and for food, energy, and consumer goods less food and energy. Within the finished-goods category, finished consumer goods account for about 76 percent of the total weight, and capital equipment for about 24 percent. Over one-third of the finished goods index is accounted for by food and energy; explosions in these particular categories (as occurred twice, for each category, in the 1970s) can drive the producer price index to extreme levels, not representative of the behavior of the whole-

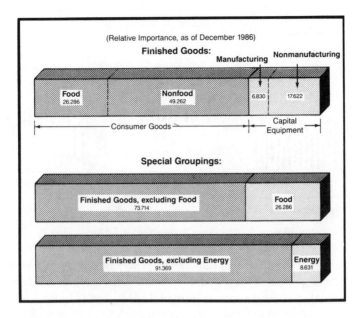

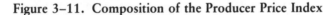

Sources: U.S. Department of Labor; The Conference Board.

Figure 3–11. Composition of the Producer Price Index

sale price level as a whole (see figure 3–11). In the 1970s, the explosions of food and energy prices drove both the consumer and wholesale price levels up very sharply. These increases were also associated with extremely rapid rises in mortgage interest rates, and the combination led to an extraordinary and partly unrepresentative explosion in the CPI as a whole, which reached close to a 20 percent inflation rate during 1974, and again in 1979–1980.

In addition to these price indexes, a multitude of indexes covering traded raw commodities are available from a variety of sources. Individual indexes within this group can behave very differently, depending on the commodities included. The behavior of these **commodity prices** is presumed to reflect world supply conditions, not just U.S. conditions; they are also—and partly for that reason—interpreted to indicate generalized tides of inflation and deflation as they affect the world economy.

The Bureau of Labor Statistics also produces a broad range of data on the earnings of Americans—most particularly, the **average hourly and weekly earnings** of employees in nonagricultural industries (see figure 3–12). The figures are available separately for manufacturing as a whole, and for a considerable range of industries within manufacturing. They are also available on a so-called constant-dollar basis—that is, after adjustment for prices—

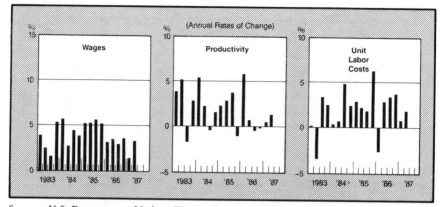

Sources: U.S. Department of Labor; The Conference Board.

Figure 3–12. The Structure of Labor Costs

that reveals trends in the real purchasing power of hourly and weekly earnings. Percentage changes in the current-dollar earnings, before adjustment for prices, are taken to be the general rate of wage increases in the United States, as reflected not in negotiated contracts but in actual hourly and weekly pay. The Bureau of Labor Statistics also compiles wage settlements above a certain size throughout the United States, and computes the average size of settlement for the first and ensuing years. But it is the monthly release on wages and their real purchasing power equivalent that makes the news.

Finally, the same energetic Bureau of Labor Statistics brings together a broad range of quarterly data on business output, hours of work, output per hour, compensation per hour, and unit labor cost for the business sector as a whole and for the business sector excluding agriculture. These are extremely valuable data even though they are available only quarterly. Most particularly, the data on output per hour represent the definitive U.S. series on the rate of gain in labor **productivity**—a crucial measure of the efficiency with which labor is being used. Moreover, if the compensation-per-hour is taken together with the output per hour, the result is a series of numbers called **unit labor cost,** which in turn is a fundamental measure of the pressures of labor cost on prices. Customarily, near the peak of the business cycle, wages are rising rapidly and productivity is declining, resulting in rapid increases in unit labor cost and hence in inflationary pressure on the price level. Early in an ensuing expansion (for example, in 1983), wages rise slowly and productivity rapidly, with the result that unit labor costs are rising slowly or not at all, and upward pressures on prices are minimal. In general, the trend of unit labor cost revealed by this series is closely related, statistically, to the behavior of the producer price index; this parallel is often drawn in charts.

Productivity measures have an importance apart from their influence on unit labor costs and prices. If export and import trends are ignored for the moment (but only for the moment: The crucial current significance of export and import trends is taken up in chapter 6), a society can consume only what it produces. Given its labor force, its output — and hence its consumption and its living standards — is determined in the end by the economic efficiency of its labor — that is, its labor productivity. The influences bearing on labor productivity include the size and quantity of the capital stock as determined by the rate of business investment in new plant and equipment (which in turn is influenced by the profitability of existing investment). They also include the educational level of the labor force, and such intangibles as the culturally determined attitude toward work and, of course, the quality of management itself. Productivity data thus provide a broad commentary on the efficiency of the entire socioeconomic structure.

Financial Data: The Capital Markets

The United States is absolutely deluged with financial data on a daily basis: The prices on an awesome range of financial assets — stocks, bonds, mutual funds, options, commodity and financial futures, even stock indexes, and even futures contracts on stock indexes — are reported daily and even hourly. This immense flow, occupying a dozen pages or so in every daily newspaper, is the inescapable daily reading of individual and institutional investors. The flow tells what is happening to the values of the enormous range of financial instruments now available to the investor. It represents the broad surface of U.S. financial markets.

Standing underneath this surface, and in many ways dictating its behavior, is the U.S. capital market, in which the price trends of securities are shaped and driven. The U.S. capital market is far and away the largest in the world; and its attractions — its liquidity and efficiency, as well as its enormous size — make it the overwhelming preoccupation of financial investors all over the world. To tap the demand, U.S. financial organizations — banks, investment bankers, brokers — have established themselves in all the other major financial markets (there are more U.S. banks in London than there are British banks). The whole world's financial market now participates globally through electronic and data systems. The world has become one huge financial market, and the U.S. market is its major national component.

The stream of information on the U.S. capital market is provided by a number of U.S. economic agencies, but by far the overwhelming share of the data emerges from the Federal Reserve System. The absolutely fundamental published source is the so-called **flow-of-funds** data system released quarterly by that agency. Unfortunately, the preparation time is long; the release generally appears several months after the end of the quarter to which it applies. It is nevertheless the crucial underpinning of any understanding of the U.S. capital market, and the behavior of its participants.

The flow-of-funds data describe, in the first instance, who has supplied capital to the market, and who has drawn it out. Summary statistics are available for each of the major sectors—the household sector, the business sector, the government sector, and the rest of the world—and by form of financial instrument: stock issue and purchase, bond issue and purchase, mortgage issue and purchase. Separate tables reveal the activity of the nonfinancial sector, the financial sector, and the aggregate. Taken together, the tables in the flow of funds are a vast sources-and-uses accounting system for the U.S. capital market. Like any such system, the sources, conceptually, equal the uses, although they are separated by a statistical discrepancy.

Drawing on these aggregate flows, the Federal Reserve constructs flows for individual sectors, of which the most significant and most widely used is the structure of accounts for the household sector (see figure 3–13). The table on households and their behavior provides a far clearer picture of their financial transactions than can be derived from the simple statements of income, spending, and aggregate saving that are provided by the national accounts. Here we get a detailed portrait of personal saving and of the repositories (by kind of financial asset) into which the saving is flowing. The tables also provide detailed measures of the net increases in personal debt—in the form of short-term consumer credit, mortgages, trade debt, and securities debt. The accounts for the corporate sector provide measures of gross investment

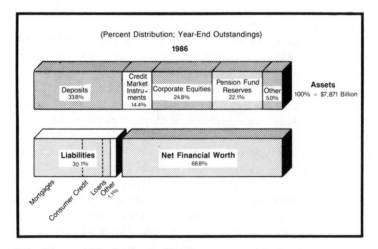

Sources: Federal Reserve; The Conference Board.

Figure 3–13. Household Assets and Liabilities

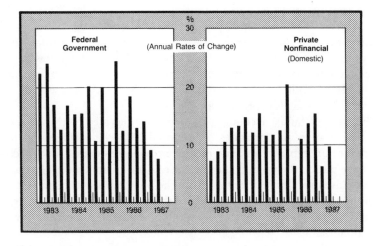

Sources: Federal Reserve; The Conference Board.

Figure 3–14. Growth Rates of Debt Outstanding

in physical assets and details of changes in the financial positions of corporations — the changes in their holdings of the whole range of liquid assets in which corporations keep their liquid funds. Comparable tables cover state and local governments and the federal government itself.

The bulk of material appearing in the flow-of-funds releases deals, naturally, with dollar increases and decreases in the holdings of financial assets. A summary table in each release relates these changes to the underlying stock of debt; that is, it relates increases or reductions in debt to the volume of debt outstanding, for the system as a whole and for five principal sectors (see figure 3–14). The table focuses powerfully on what may be the central statistic of the capital market: the **growth rates of debt outstanding.**

To calculate the growth rates of outstanding debt requires a balance-sheet measure of the *level* of debt. Once a year (but unfortunately with a lag running to as much as ten months) the Federal Reserve produces a balance-sheet statement of **outstanding assets and liabilities** for the system as a whole and for each of the sectors. The tables in this annual issue deal with outstanding credit market debt at year end; they provide a fundamental measure of the debt structure according to who owes the debt and the form of instruments in which it is embodied.

Equity securities are not a form of debt, of course, but a substantial portion of household wealth appears in this form and is carried in the count of total financial assets in the household sector. Their value before the 1987 crash was over $2 trillion, double the level of 1980, and three times the level of 1975 (but as much as $800 billion was lost in the 1987 crash). Other useful figures: The household sector owns about $800 billion of U.S. securities; pension fund reserves now equal $2 trillion. The total financial assets of the household sector, including their holdings of equities as well as of fixed-income assets, is now about $8 trillion, and their liabilities are approximately $3 trillion. The net financial worth of U.S. households is thus still over $5 trillion. It's a rich country.

The flow-of-funds accounting system is integrated with the national accounting system and provides an essential financial background for the flows of output, expenditure, and income provided by the national accounts. As with the national accounts, the volume of detail is immense. The quarterly release receives very little attention from the business press, but an examination of the accounts as they appear (the release is available directly from the Federal Reserve) always provides additional insights into the behavior of the financial markets.

Some of the innumerable financial series contained within the flow-of-funds accounts are maintained in more current condition (that is, monthly) or in greater detail, by the U.S. Treasury in its monthly *Treasury Bulletin,* and by the Federal Reserve in its monthly *Federal Reserve Bulletin.* The Treasury is, of course, home base for the description of Treasury debt. Available from the Treasury are tabulations of the entire debt structure, by coupon and maturity, as well as ongoing monthly data on federal outlay and receipts, in greater detail than is available anywhere else. Their issuance rarely makes the news, even though they are of profound interest to dealers in the markets for federal securities. The *Federal Reserve Bulletin* provides a large number of tables on the condition of **capital markets,** including sections on the condition of the commercial banking system, interest rates, terms of lending at commercial banks, the stock market, and federal fiscal and financing operations. Very few of these figures are released to the press, and still fewer receive any press attention. For readers active in the financial markets, the details in the *Federal Reserve Bulletin* are a rich source of information on the market's behavior.

The Securities and Exchange Commission (SEC) issues a monthly statistical review that provides detail on the value and volume of equity transactions on U.S. exchanges as well as on option markets, public offerings of new securities, and new-security registrations with the Commission. Again, the monthly bulletin produces no figures that receive much attention in the press; the materials it contains are primarily of interest to traders and professionals in the equity market and in investment banking.

4
How to Watch the Business Cycle

The long history of the U.S. economy, as well as of all other developed market economies, reveals a persistent tendency toward alternating periods of expansion and contraction that together are called the **business cycle.** In fact, long-term economic history, as it appears in broad indicators of economic behavior, can be broken down into an oscillating *cyclical* component; imposed on a long-term growth *trend;* all confused and made difficult to deal with in the short run because of *irregular,* unsystematic, random movements. A schematic illustration of these three types of movement in isolation, and then combined into the living reality of a typical economic series, is seen in figure 4–1. Figure 4–2 shows the long-term history of expansions and contractions in the economy, as determined by the National Bureau of Economic Research, the unofficial but widely respected custodian of business-cycle statistics for the United States.

There are a number of good reasons why a sensitive, interconnected aggregate, shot through with feedbacks from one part of the system to another, should experience a tide of change in one direction, a reversal, and then a tide of change in the other direction, alternately reaching a peak at the end of an expansion, and a trough at the end of a recession. The tide is familiar enough to virtually all businessmen, who sense it in their own operations as the conditions confronting them go from strong uptrend, to uncertainty, to strong downtrend; and then on into renewed uncertainty, and then improvement. The tide is repetitive—*cyclical.*

Each business-cycle experience is unique; it takes its duration, its rates of change, and its shape from always unique combinations of the raw materials on which it works, the position of fiscal and monetary policy, legislative changes, accidents of weather, military and other international conditions, and so on. Although each occurrence is unique, the cyclical experience itself draws on several inherent characteristics of modern economies. The characteristics responsible for the business cycle can be modified somewhat—and offset somewhat—by deliberate government effort, but a modern economy will experience the business cycle in important degree as long as it retains a predominantly free-market system.

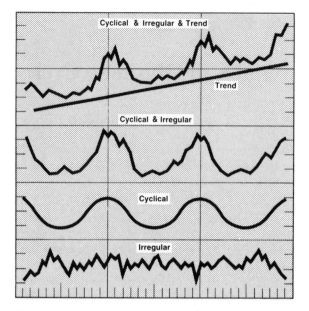

Source: The Conference Board.

Figure 4–1. The Components of Statistical Movement

The final expression of demand for all the products and services on the market—the culmination of an economic process in the profitable sale of a good to a willing buyer—draws on a complicated chain of resources and activities that brings the final product in touch with the demand. The supply chain by which an automobile is brought to a dealership for ultimate sale is traceable back through an endless supply chain of fabricated components, and thence back to an enormous range of raw-materials industries—rubber, steel, nonferrous metals, glass, fibers, and so on (see figure 4–3). Changes in the demand for automobiles, as expressed by the sales of dealers, send a demand impulse back along this long and complex chain, giving rise to changes in ordering rates as it goes. The more complex the product, typically, the more complex the trail of change. The impact of change at the ultimate point of sale thus sets in motion a *time-consuming* process of adjustment, in the same direction. A change in demand, for whatever reason, is not an event but an alteration of a rhythm—a shock wave that travels down a long and sensitive line of subdemands within the business system. As the energy is transmitted through these channels, in time it also alters (again, in the same direction) the investment intentions and inventory policies of the industries involved.

The complex supply chains that are characteristic of modern economic systems give us reason enough to expect that the system as a whole will

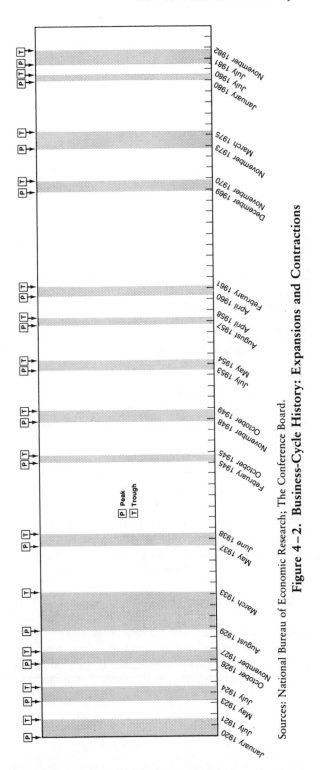

Sources: National Bureau of Economic Research; The Conference Board.

Figure 4–2. Business-Cycle History: Expansions and Contractions

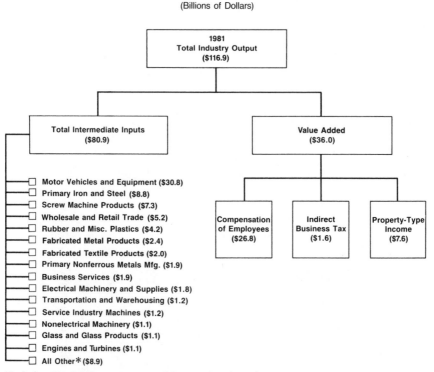

(Billions of Dollars)

*Includes 52 miscellaneous commodities not elsewhere shown.

Sources: U.S. Department of Commerce; The Conference Board.

Figure 4–3. A Simplified Supply Chain for the Motor-Vehicle Industry

engage in sustained movements, up or down, until other forces enter the equation. But another characteristic mechanism of modern societies tends to reinforce the cyclical consequences of long supply chains. In modern economies, production is responsible for most of the generation of income. Rising demand for output yields rising output, and the rising output elevates the very income variables that are responsible for the rising demand. An economy experiencing an expanding level of demand is *always* experiencing an expanding level of income, and hence, at least for a time, *further* increment to the demand.

In contrast with the supply-chain effect described here, which operates on only one side of the market, this production-income link can be thought of as a continuous positive feedback leading from more (less) production, to more (less) income, to more (less) demand, to more (less) production.

This process acquires special significance if the change in demand is for plant and equipment and/or inventory—goods that go into the system's balance sheet rather than its operating statement. Higher demand for these *balance-sheet* goods creates income (in the course of their production) that flows into the *operating-statement* markets for consumer goods, creating additional production, and therefore additional income, and therefore, of course, additional demand. This effect is called a *multiplier;* it means that a dollar of incremental demand for investment goods may yield about three dollars of aggregate increase in the total GNP.

Another related mechanism that tends to augment the strength and durability of business-cycle movements relates to the presence of very large markets for long-lived durable goods—a distinguishing feature of highly developed economies. The market for very long-lived goods is characterized by a very low relationship of oncoming supply to the existing stock. For example, refrigerators last, say, ten years on average. To maintain the existing stock of refrigerators, annual production amounting to only one-tenth of the stock is required. If, for any reason, the market desires a 10 percent increase in the stock, the tendency for output is to double—that is, to provide the output required to maintain the existing stock, and *then* the output required to elevate it to the new desired level. The longer the good lasts, the lower the percentage relationship of oncoming supply to the existing stock, and the more volatile the production response to a change in the desired stock. This *stock-flow* principle explains the extreme amplitude of the production cycle for houses, automobiles, office buildings, and major machinery. (In its application particularly to machinery, the principle is called the *accelerator.*) This characteristic tends to enlarge the amplitude of the business cycle, though perhaps without altering its timing.

Particularly with respect to investment goods, modern economies experience powerful positive feedbacks from the business cycle in the demand for general goods to a business cycle in the demand for the plant and equipment that produces them—the multiplier and the accelerator at work. As operating rates in general industry rise, margins of available capacity dwindle, and the efforts of individual companies to provide for further growth—and to protect their share of market—will require them to accelerate the entire cycle by increasing their orders for nonresidential structures and machinery and, probably, for inventory as well.

Thus there are large numbers of plain reasons that a system constructed in the way this one is should experience strong tides of expansion, reinforcing themselves as they go; and then, in reverse, strong tides of contraction that also tend to persevere, to spread, and to grow deeper as they go. Of course, business-cycle expansions do not continue indefinitely, and recessions do not collapse the system down to zero economic activity. The question remains: Why do expansions finally reach a climax, during which the business trend suddenly stabilizes and then reverses into recession; and why do recessions lose their energy, and finally give way to renewed expansion?

In addition to the machinery within the economic system that extends and intensifies movement in any one direction, there are also limiting and restraining structures that drag increasingly on the business-cycle movement, and finally dominate and reverse it. Among the structural reasons for the system to act in this retardant way is the simple proposition that increments to the available supply of *anything* must finally experience declining utility. In the course of a business expansion, the eleventh unit of addition to the stock of consumer goods has a lower utility than the tenth unit; as personal spending continues to rise during an expansion, the *marginal* value of further *spending* declines, while the *marginal* value of *saving* rises. The *marginal propensity to spend* thus declines in the course of a business expansion, whereas the *marginal propensity to save* rises, and an increasing share of personal income finds its way into financial assets, rather than the real assets represented in the final demand of consumers as measured in the GNP. The tendency for spending to lose its energy, and for saving to grow, is often intensified in the late stages of the business cycle by higher interest rates, which restrict the incentive to borrow in order to spend, and increase the reward for saving.

The accounts of the federal government also tend to constrain the energy of the business cycle and gradually to arrest its movement. In the course of a business expansion, government revenues tend to rise more rapidly than GNP itself because of the presence of the progressive personal tax structure. (The indexation of tax brackets effective in 1985 reduces this effect.) At the same time, government expenditures, which are budgeted in dollars, are not importantly influenced by the business cycle. (Certain forms of social outlay, such as unemployment compensation, are even likely to decline as employment conditions improve.)

The net position of the federal government in the course of a business expansion thus ordinarily moves from deficit toward balance, and the stimulus provided by the deficit in the government account thus shrinks. Conversely, in the course of a recession, the government's income falls, whereas its expenditures are largely unchanged (often, in fact, they increase as a result of efforts to offset recession). The federal deficit thus tends to widen as activity in the system subsides. The net budget position of the federal government is thus a countervailing, anticyclical influence on the behavior of the system as a whole, even in the absence of any consciously contracyclical behavior on the part of the government itself. Of course, the contracyclical position of the government is often reinforced by deliberate behavior; that is, tax increases almost always occur during expansions, and tax reductions during recessions. Monetary policy, too, tends to tighten (thereby inducing rises in interest rates) during expansions and to relax (thereby producing more abundant supplies of credit and lower interest rates) during recessions.

Finally, inventory conditions often provide the climactic event that reverses the business cycle from an expansion phase to a contraction phase, and vice versa. As final demands grow more slowly in the late stage of an expansion (remember the diminishing utility of increments to output), inventories tend to grow at the same time that higher interest rates increase the cost of carrying the inventory. Inventory accumulation finally becomes unintended, then reluctant, and finally flatly involuntary and undesired. The effort to slow inventory growth, however, means reducing orders to suppliers, who reduce *their* orders to their suppliers, and so on down the long chain of supply described earlier. The effort to curtail inventory is often the crucial reverser of the business cycle into recession; conversely, the effort to reverse an undesired decline in inventory often converts recession into renewed expansion.

The Cycle in the Statistics

The business cycle is a broad, all-encompassing tide within the business system. Although its focus is in goods industries (in part because that is where the inventory mechanism is at work) few industries — and therefore few statistical series — escape it entirely. Its more apparent statistical influences are described here; but practically any industry association, and for that matter any individual company, will find the cycle embedded, in varying degrees of intensity, in its own statistical record.

Because it is such a broad and pervasive phenomenon, the cycle is plainly visible in the record of the national accounts themselves. Figure 4–4 shows the behavior of various components of expenditure and income, as measured in the GNP, in the course of several business cycles (the shaded areas in the charts represent the periods of recession and the unshaded areas the periods of expansion). It is apparent from the chart that considerable parts of the GNP do not seem to experience the business cycle in any significant degree; government demand grows in recession and expansion alike, and personal outlays for services appear to operate largely independently of the general business conditions imposed by the cycle.

On the other hand, some components of the GNP react very clearly — and some of them explosively — to changes in the cyclical phase of the system. These highly susceptible components are, in general, those components where credit formation plays an important part in total demand; and those components, mainly of an investment nature, that involve long-lived durable goods — those for which purchases can be deferred during times of uncertainty, followed by a catching up of demand in times of prosperity (activating the stock-flow principle described earlier). These susceptible components are consumer-durables outlays (long-lived, and heavily dependent on installment credit); the outlays of business for plant and equipment (also long-lived, also credit-dependent); residential building (again long-lived and credit-

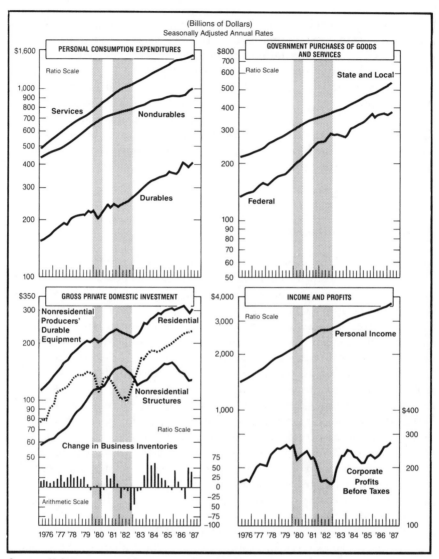

Sources: U.S. Department of Commerce; The Conference Board.

Figure 4–4. Cyclical Behavior in the National Accounts

dependent); and changes in business inventories (not long-lived, of course, but highly sensitive to the expectations of business with respect to future business volume and prices, and very sensitive to interest-rate developments because the carrying cost of inventory is largely a function of the prevailing short-term interest rate).

Since the sensitivity of the various parts of the GNP to business-cycle conditions differs so much among the components, the internal composition of the GNP changes with the stages of the business cycle. In fact, the internal composition moves in very much the same rhythm as the business cycle itself. Figure 4–5 adds together those parts of the GNP that are most responsive to the cycle, and expresses this subtotal as a percentage of total GNP. At the bottom of a recession, the share of the total GNP taken by these sensitive markets is predictably low; it rises in the course of the expansion, reaches a peak just prior to the onset of recession, and then subsides again to its next recessionary trough.

This compositional view of the GNP carries a high information content for forecasting because it describes whether the structure of the system is already very far advanced into expansion and increasingly sensitive to recession, or whether it is compressed into the typical defensive position of recession and prepared to respond vigorously to the early stages of a new expansion.

The national-accounts components are highly aggregated, they deal only with matters of final sale, and the bulk of them are available only quarterly.

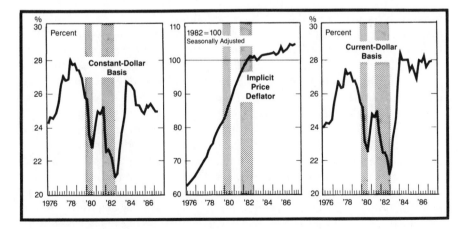

Note: Cyclical share consists of Gross Private Domestic Investment and Durables PCE as percent of Gross National Produce.

Sources: U.S. Department of Commerce; The Conference Board.

Figure 4–5. The Cyclical Share of Output

For that reason, their value in analyzing the business cycle is limited, and they need to be supplemented by more sensitive indicators, often dealing with orders, production, spending intentions, commitments to future activities— cyclically sensitive data that are available on a monthly basis. Many such useful data have been described in preceding sections; here some of them are brought together, particularly in the context of the business cycle.

One standard approach to appraising the phase of the business cycle is to study individual indicators whose past behavior suggests a stable relationship to the business cycle as a whole. Research by the National Bureau of Economic Research and others has identified a large number of readily available economic series that tend to lead the general business cycle; that is, they reach their peaks and troughs before general business and thereby provide, at least, an alert to the probability of a change in the direction of the cycle. Other indicators found in the same search have a record of coinciding very closely with the business cycle itself, and still others exhibit a characteristic lag; that is, they reach their peaks and troughs *after* the general business cycle. The three sets of series are called leading, coincident, and lagging series. In an idealized experience with them, the leading series would pass through a turning point, followed by the coincident series, and then—in a final confirmatory signal—by the lagging series.

The behavior of some of these series over the past several cycles is shown in figure 4–6. It does not take a very practiced statistical eye to detect a difficulty with this useful but simple forecasting instrument. The series that lead the general business cycle are, in general, much more erratic in their month-to-month behavior than are the coincident or lagging series, and it is therefore much harder to establish a high probability that they are indicating a turning point in the business cycle. Any businessman will recognize that a series expressing new orders will be much more volatile than one expressing actual ongoing production. Even allowing for the talents of modern computers, the difficulty is inescapable: The series with the longest (and therefore most valuable) leads behave most problematically. There are not that many of them, in any event; the business cycle is so pervasive a phenomenon that the great bulk of the available monthly statistical series reach their turning points at very nearly the same time. Nevertheless, the indicator approach to observing the business cycle has distinct value, and the series are watched even by forecasters who also pay a great deal of attention to other devices.

A second approach to observing the business cycle is to focus not so much on how rapidly business conditions are improving or deteriorating, but on how *widespread* the rises or declines in statistical series may be—not on the rate of change of aggregate business, but on the *dispersion* of trends within the aggregate. When aggregate business activity is rising, one would expect that a majority of a reasonably representative collection of indicators would also be rising; when the aggregate system is declining, one would

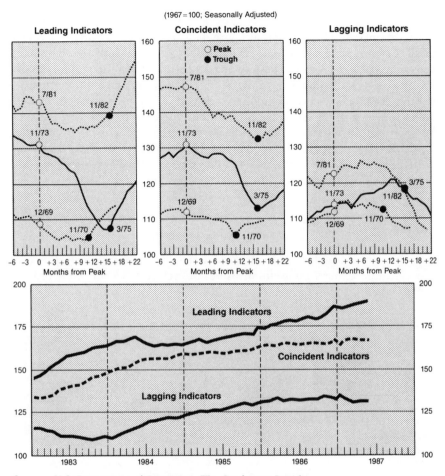

Sources: U.S. Department of Commerce; The Conference Board.

Figure 4–6. Indicators of Business-Cycle Behavior

expect that more than half of such a representative collection would be falling; and when total business activity is moving sideways (a rare occurrence, and rarely sustained for any length of time), one would expect that about the same number of activities are declining as are rising. This approach studies the dispersion of activity among large numbers of indicators, or their *diffusion*. (A business parallel would be the behavior of a large conglomerate with many more or less unrelated divisions; in an expanding economy, more than half the divisions would be doing very well, whereas in a declining economy more than half of them would be expected to be doing poorly.)

A number of agencies attempt to capture this sense of dispersion or diffusion in the system by measuring the disparity, in a large number of statistical series, between the number rising and the number falling. The Conference Board's **diffusion index,** shown in figure 4–7, is one such effort. It is composed of twenty series, some of them measuring industrial activities and some measuring trade activities. The principal index measures the percentage of the total series that appear to be rising. The Commerce Department's monthly **leading indicator composite,** released about four weeks after the month to which it applies, receives enormous attention from the press. Like the approach through individual indicators, such a device is far from foolproof; yet it does carry information about the width of activities experiencing positive and negative business-cycle trends, and has carried imprecise but useful leading characteristics.

Foreshadowing Statistics

By their nature, a number of statistical series *foreshadow* future business activity, and are therefore useful measures of cyclical tendency. New orders

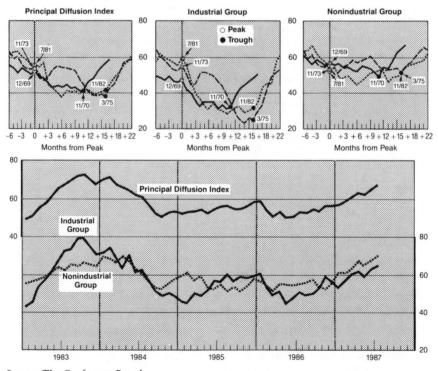

Source: The Conference Board.

Figure 4–7. The Behavior of the Diffusion Index

in manufacturing industries forecast the production to satisfy the orders; construction contract awards forecast the construction activity in fulfillment of a contract; new incorporations foreshadow the acquisition of basic equipment by new enterprises. The federal budget itself is a foreshadowing statistic, since there flows from it a stream of budgetary authorizations, appropriations, and obligations that amount to new orders for the goods and services purchased by government. Several of the series referred to as *leading indicators* carry these characteristics.

Foreshadowing statistics have a contractual character, in that foregoing the implied activity carries a cost (the cost of escaping from the contract). Their connection to the business cycle is *causal,* not just statistical. Upstream from these more or less committed orders and contracts are *expectations* series—in general, surveys of *anticipated* outlay, whose findings are not necessarily restricted to contractual obligations.

Consumers are now heavily surveyed with respect to their attitudes, their satisfaction with their financial condition, their personal expectations for the future, and even their buying plans for individual consumer products. Businessmen are surveyed, by the U.S. Department of Commerce and others, for their expected rate of outlay on **plant and equipment** as much as six months to a year ahead, without regard to the proportion of the plans already embedded in firm orders to contractors and machinery producers. Such planned purchases and outlays by consumers and businesses are before the fact, and they can be withdrawn from without cost. They are thus much more erratic and less dependable. They nevertheless retain considerable utility, and are closely observed. Figures 4–8 and 4–9 indicate the behavior of a typical survey of consumer attitudes in the course of a business cycle, and the behavior of the U.S. Department of Commerce survey of businessmen's anticipated outlays for plant and equipment.

Other Indicators of the Cycle

The business cycle, as noted, makes its appearance most powerfully among a selected group of markets—those markets that are credit-related and that are composed of relatively big ticket and long-lived goods. These are the same markets whose aggregate behavior, expressed as a share of GNP, describes the stage of the cycle in terms of the composition of output. This aggregate behavior of components of the national accounts appears in figure 4–4, but there are a large number of *monthly* statistics bearing on these markets that add important short-term information on the development of the cycle. Some of these series appear in figure 4–10 (for a period in which no business-cycle turning point has been identified). They include sales rates for automobiles and major household goods, construction starts of residential buildings, machinery ordering rates, and the ongoing monthly change in business inven-

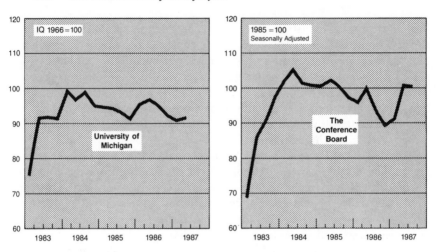

Sources: University of Michigan; The Conference Board.

Figure 4–8. Two Measures of Consumer Sentiment

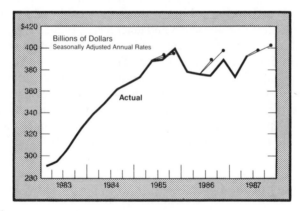

•Anticipated.

Note: Extensions of actual plottings are anticipated outlays as of mid-year.

Sources: U.S. Department of Commerce; The Conference Board.

Figure 4–9. Anticipated Capital Outlays

tories. Each of these series is a sensitive monthly reflection of an ongoing investment activity, generally involving extension of credit and hence reflecting the degree of confidence in the future of buyers (both businesses and consumers). The changes in direction of these series mark important points in the progress of the business cycle simply as a matter of rising and falling fundamental demands, but they also reflect changing attitudes—the flux of collective judgment about the future.

The stock market itself is among the most sensitive and prescient indi-

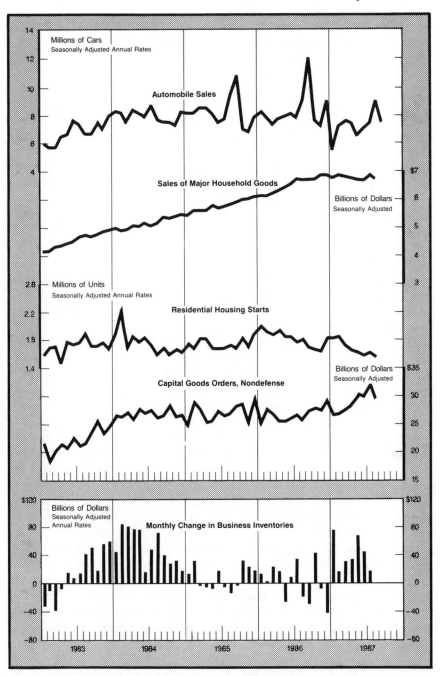

Sources: Ward's Automotive Reports; U.S. Department of Commerce; The Conference Board.

Figure 4–10. Selected Cyclical Indicators

cators of collective attitudes. In connection with the stock market, it should be noted that major moves in the **values of securities** do not represent simply a forecasting or expectational variable. Important changes in the values of securities have a powerful influence on the balance sheet of the household sector; at present, for example, every point in the Dow Jones Index is approximately the equivalent of $1.2 billion in personal wealth. The rise and fall of securities prices thus produces a tide of *wealth effects* in the form of realized and unrealized capital gains and losses experienced by the holders. The stock market does not simply *forecast* changes in business conditions; in some degree, it *causes* them, through inflation and deflation of the personal balance sheet and, hence, of the attitudes of the consumer sector as a whole.

Finally, the list of key business-cycle statistics includes **interest rates.** Discussion of federal-government policies that influence rates appears in chapter 5; here it is essential to note that fluctuations in rates are powerfully related to the business cycle of the past dozen years. Sharp elevations in interest rates deter buyers and increase the reward for saving; they are thus a major constricting force on business conditions. Conversely, substantial reductions in interest rates lower the cost of credit-oriented purchases and reduce the alternative reward (interest income) for withholding funds from consumption. Ever since 1980, as figure 4–11 reveals, the general level of interest rates has had a powerful correlation with the aggregate business cycle. A related indicator that is highly suggestive with respect to oncoming cyclical conditions is the real value of the money stock—that is, the money stock converted to a measure of purchasing power through "deflation" by an index of price trends. The rate of change of this purchasing power measure tends to precede changes in general business conditions (see figure 4–12).

The indicators described in this section make up the regular diet of business-cycle analysis and forecasting. Each appearance of a new number in these series is searched for its cyclical significance. For long stretches of months, quarters, and even years, these indicators typically throw off signs of continuing growth in economic activity; then they gradually lose their coherence as conflicting trends become visible among them; finally—often in a period measured only in weeks—the general impression of cyclical stage conveyed by the numbers changes dramatically, and the consensus of forecasters, moved by the accumulating evidence, begins to reach toward a forecast of recession. As the impression spreads, attitudes throughout the system respond; the response itself enlarges caution and introduces still more powerful hesitations into the concerned markets. The climactic moment of the business cycle occurs when a trend reverses and the awareness of the reversal spreads throughout the business, financial, and consumer community— altering general expectations, inducing a search for shelter, and inaugurating the pursuit of security and liquidity. Anticipating such a turning point effectively, or at least recognizing it promptly, is a necessary and rewarding part of short-term and intermediate-term business planning.

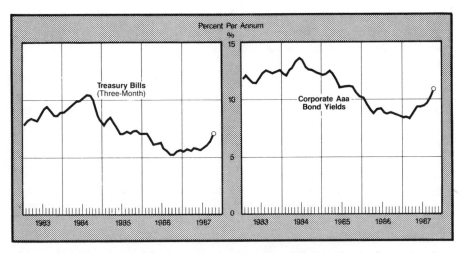

Sources: U.S. Department of the Treasury; Moody's Investors Service; The Conference Board.

Figure 4–11. The Cycle in Interest Rates

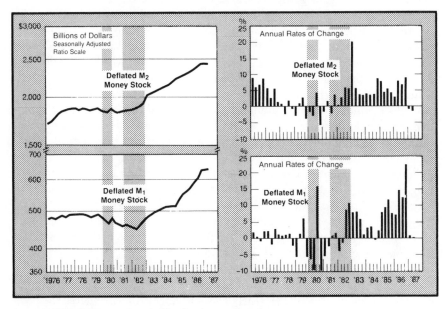

Sources: Federal Reserve Board; The Conference Board.

Figure 4–12. The Cycle in Purchasing Power of Money

The business-cycle machinery described here is ineradicably present in a free-market system. The cycle subsists in the form of alternating energies—a pendulum-like exchange of potentials from one state (recession) to an ensuing reverse state (expansion). Staying with the pendulum simile, it is possible to envision sets of circumstances that would arrest its motion, or make it so wobbly and arrhythmic as to give it the appearance of almost random behavior.

The environment in which the pendulum operates can be so viscous, so clouded with particular circumstances and criss-cross trends, that the exchange of energy becomes impossible, and the business cycle is stilled even though the mechanism is intact. This stilling of a cycle, and the suspension of many of the indications of cyclical behavior described in this chapter, is strikingly visible in the experience of U.S. business since the middle of 1984, when a strong cyclical recovery from the strong recession of 1981–1982 seemed to come to a halt. Three years after this sudden arresting of the cycle, little or no cyclical energy is visible. In late 1987, it was often observed by economic forecasters that the business-cycle expansion had reached a duration of five years (measuring from its beginnings at the bottom of recession in late 1982). But the last three years of this period do not look like business-cycle behavior at all; on the contrary, they appear as uncoordinated drift, with individual markets (including the great cyclical markets themselves) operating at cross purposes, as though their basic interconnections had been severed.

In its application to forecasting, economic reasoning, and particularly business-cycle reasoning, have been utterly frustrated. Huge budget deficits have not turned out to be stimulative; the inflation rate, which normally rises during an expansion, has fallen (at least until very recently); interest rates, which customarily rise in the late stages of expansion, have fallen dramatically (again, until recently); abundant availability of credit has fueled explosive behavior in financial markets, while the real world has drifted along placidly. The pendulum has stopped, slightly to the positive side of dead center.

There are two great, and taken together quite sufficient, explanations for the noncyclical character of business in recent years. In the first place, the long trajectories of debt, physical holdings of goods, and international competitive position described in chapter 1 have deposited heavy anticyclical weights on the system. They have dulled the normal responses of borrowing and investing that are fundamental parts of the business cycle. Second, the fundamental change in the U.S. position with respect to the rest of the world—most particularly, the fall of the dollar over the two years ending in the middle of 1987, and the incredible surge of imports (partly a reflection of the elevation of the dollar in the early 1980s)—have radically altered the position of the manufacturing sector in the system. Manufacturing output, investment, and even inventory policy have been profoundly weakened by the flood of imports from the developed world (Europe and Japan), as well as from a host of newly industrialized countries (South Korea, Taiwan, and Hong Kong, for example). In the presence of these huge tides, one in our own domestic history and the other in our place in the world, the wave of the business cycle is hard to find out there.

But despite the confusion of the evidence, a revival of the business cycle, in both its expansion and recession phases, is an expectable future development. The structure of the cycle, as described in this chapter, is unalterably present. It would be a mistake to assume that the force of the cycle, always formidable when it gathers strength, will not reappear in time. The pendulum is still, but the machinery is there, to be restarted when conditions again favor a return to traditional patterns of free-market behavior.

5
The Influences of Economic Policy

No businessperson or consumer in the United States (or for that matter, in any developed economy) needs to be told that government, at all its levels, exerts a powerful influence on the behavior of business. Some government policies are specific to individual industries and markets (regulatory policies, antitrust policies); some, such as environmental regulation, accept general economic costs in order to achieve partly noneconomic objectives. Others seek to influence the relationship of the U.S. economy to its trading partners and the rest of the world; still others pursue long-term distributive goals (fair and just distribution of income, elimination of poverty, improved health, job security, higher educational standards) set by ethical considerations as much as by supposed economic benefit. Each of government's multiple objectives, and how well or ill its efforts serve those objectives, is a study in itself not appropriately pursued here.

Beyond these specific economic and social goals, however, the government carries a large *general* economic mandate to seek and maintain an economic environment in which *general* economic activity prospers — an environment in which the private sector, composed of private individuals and private corporations, can pursue economic interest in a favorable climate of general growth and stability. The mandate and the responsibility are not new: they developed informally, and without an explicit legislative base, during the Great Depression of the 1930s. The legislative base — the explicit commitment — was put in place in the early postwar years. That legislation, embodied in the Employment Act of 1946, intended to state that henceforth government would use its economic powers to ensure that nothing like the 1930s would occur again.

In pursuit of this general objective, the federal government possesses two powerful sets of economic instruments broadly characterized as *fiscal policy* and *monetary policy*. The two arms of policy can work together to supplement each other when powerful stimulus or restraint is sought. Or they can work in beneficial or damaging opposition, when one or the other arm is driven off course into excessive stimulation or excessive restraint. The condition of each of the two arms of policy, and the relationship between them, are among the most powerful forces affecting the course of business in the private sector. Accordingly, the statistics reflecting these conditions are vital and essential guides to the future of business itself.

Fiscal Policy

Fiscal policy means, most generally, the influences on the private sector emanating from the condition of the federal budget—the spending of the federal government, its receipts, its surplus or deficit, and the resultant accumulating debt. Unlike many other sovereign governments, and unlike many of the U.S. state governments, the federal government does not engage in capital accounting. Its operations are recorded very nearly as a cash flow—cash income, less cash outgo (no balance sheet, no reporting of depreciation of long-lived assets, no net worth or stockholders' equity). When the government buys something, it treats the purchase as a cash outlay, ignoring the asset value of what it bought; when it sells something, it treats the proceeds as income, disregarding the reduction in its holdings of assets.

As this may not be the best way to run a railroad, so it is not necessarily the best way to run a government (there are many sophisticated studies of how the accounting might be improved, some of which are being gradually embodied in proposed legislation). But that's the way it is, and that's what the currently available figures mean. A surplus in the federal budget (a very rare occurrence since the 1920s, when a surplus was mandated by law) simply means that the government is experiencing an infusion of cash, which it uses to pay back a portion of its outstanding debt (actually, it means the government is issuing less debt than it is retiring). A deficit (a much more familiar phenomenon) means the government is experiencing a cash drain, which it finances by issuing additional debt instruments (that is, issuing new debt instruments faster than it is redeeming old instruments). The debt instruments of the federal government are absolutely risk-free with respect to the payment of principal and interest (but not necessarily in terms of current value, since the market value of longer-term issues will fluctuate with general interest rates). Being what might be called interest-bearing cash, the increased issuance of government securities enlarges the supply of cash and near-cash in the hands of the private sector, and is therefore, almost without exception, treated by economists as a stimulus to private business. The record of all this almost continuous stimulus is shown in figure 5–1, which records the spending, receipts, and deficit or surplus of the federal government, and the accumulation of debt instruments by which the debt has been financed, all on a fiscal-year basis (the federal government is now on an October 1–September 30 fiscal year).

Because deficits are considered stimulative in any first-round analysis,

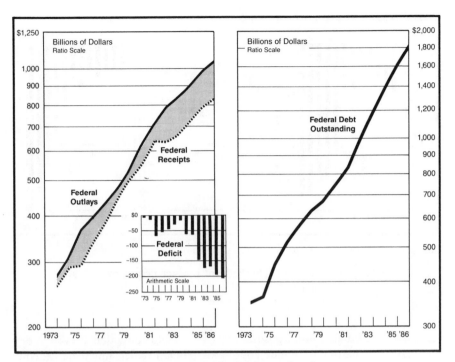

Sources: U.S. Department of the Treasury; The Conference Board.

Figure 5–1. Federal Receipts, Outlays, and Debt

they are generally thought to be appropriate at times when the economy appears to need stimulus. This is most particularly true, of course, during general recession with its accompanying unemployment. Historically, the big deficits have been experienced precisely during recession, simply because during recessions private incomes fall, and therefore the revenues of the federal government decline, whereas budgeted spending is unaffected by recession (the effect of recession on spending is generally to enlarge it through higher unemployment-compensation payments and other deliberately stimulative spending efforts). Deficits produced in this way are often called *passive* deficits, or **cyclical deficits,** because they result mainly not from intentional policy moves but as a reaction to recession itself. In an important sense, such deficits *measure* the severity of the recession and *cushion* the private sector as it declines.

Since nobody particularly likes recession, the deficits experienced in the course of one are often deliberately accentuated by tax reduction (which further suppresses government revenues) or by deliberate *contracyclical* spending programs. Even in the absence of recession, tax reductions (such as those instituted by the Reagan Administration) and/or spending increases

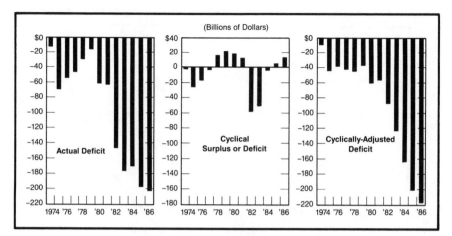

Sources: U.S. Department of Commerce; The Conference Board.

Figure 5–2. The Federal Budget Position

can drive the budget into a position where it would run a deficit even under generally prosperous economic conditions. Such a deficit might be called a *secular* or *structural* deficit, or a **cyclically adjusted deficit.** Economists have struggled for decades to achieve separate measures of the *cyclical* and the *structural* deficit—that is, the part of the deficit that simply results from underemployment and recession in the private economy, and the part that reflects the real longer-term position of the deficit attributable to the tax rates imposed by the federal government and its spending—a mismatch of the expectable revenues from the tax structure, on the one hand, and the spending intentions on the other hand. The latest effort at this calculation, which yields a cyclical deficit and a cyclically adjusted deficit (the secular deficit) appear in figure 5–2. (The aggregate recent history of the deficit, as calculated in the national accounts, was discussed in chapter 2.)

The difference between the cyclical deficit and the secular or structural deficit is crucial to appraising the budget position. By definition, the cyclical deficit reflects the presence of idle resources; the stimulus provided by the deficit can be expressed in rising real production activity. The structural deficit, however, already adjusted to high employment conditions, implies stimulus beyond the ability of real production to respond. It is, therefore, a probable cause of inflation in ordinary times. The fact that it did *not* cause inflation in the years 1984 to 1987 is an indication of how abnormal the times have been.

If, like most economists, we accept the proposition that budget deficits are inherently stimulative, then it is well worth looking at their present and prospective position. For almost a decade, the federal government has been required by law to produce five-year projections of revenues, expenditures,

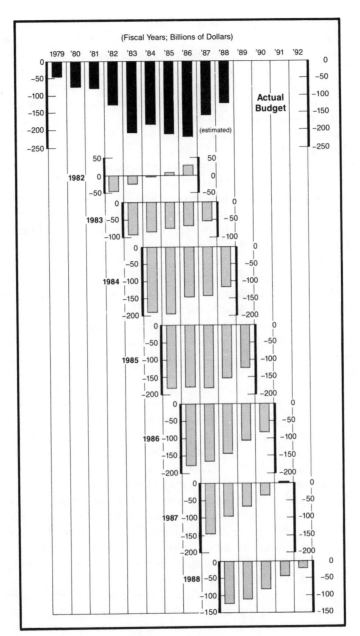

Sources: Office of Management and Budget; The Conference Board.

Figure 5–3. Five-Year Budget Projections: The New Disequilibrium

and surpluses or deficits, based on its proposed intentions with respect to taxes and outlays, and on the prospects for the state of the economy. Figure 5–3 discloses the evolution of these five-year forecasts since 1982. The picture is one of projected progress out of deficit and into surplus all the way through the 1986 budget submission; ever since, anticipated deficits rule emphatically in all the five-year projections, with some moderation in recent years. The conclusion must be that unless revenue and expenditure trends are to be altered to equal or beat the latest projections, the federal budget will be in a powerfully stimulative, perhaps ultimately inflationary, deficit position throughout the remainder of this decade.

Such an unfortunate outcome still appears to be possible as of the fall of 1987. The legislation known as Gramm-Rudman-Hollings (or, for brevity, Gramm-Rudman) expresses the intention of the Congress and of the administration to move the federal budget deficit sharply downward, to a condition of absolute neutrality—that is, a zero deficit—by 1991. But the powers to "sequester" funds and programs, ultimately applied as across the board reductions in spending, ran into constitutional problems. New arrangements for this Draconian way of assuring shrinking deficits are less Draconian and less dependable. The Congressional Budget Office (a kind of research arm of the Congress on budgetary matters) and the Office of Management and Budget (the wing of the administration charged with the construction and defense of budgets) are in disagreement with the extent of progress that can be expected and, therefore, the need for still further legislation curtailing the growth of outlay and adding to the income side through tax increases. The projections shown in figure 5–3 for later periods are therefore much in doubt; many highly qualified private analysts of the budget position consider that the effort to reach Gramm-Rudman targets remains very uncertain.

How did a nation with perhaps the most aggressive orientation toward free markets of any country in the world develop so large a federal budget issue, particularly in the years of a Republican Administration? The answer to the paradox lies in the particular objectives of the Reagan Administration and, in some degree, their frustration by the Congress. The huge budget deficits of the past five years reflect rapidly rising outlay for defense, on the one hand, and massive reduction in personal tax rates, and hence in receipts of personal taxes, as a consequence of the rate reductions of the years 1982–1984. Reaganomics required a degree of curtailment in nondefense outlays that went far beyond the intentions of the Congress. (For the reasons for the resistance to curtailment of such outlays, see chapter 8.) Even at this writing, a half-dozen years after the issue of the budget deficit began to assume its present shape and importance, the Congress and the admininstration are still deeply divided over how much of the deficit gap should be closed by spending restraint, and how much through reimposition of taxes.

Monetary Policy

Turn now to the second great arm of national economic policy—the **monetary conditions** imposed on the system by the Federal Reserve. The Fed, as it is affectionately known to the financial community, is a great and powerful, largely independent (but ultimately a creature of Congress) system of control over the creation of credit in the system—particularly the commercial banks' power to lend to the private sector and, of course, to government itself.

The creation of credit is a complex and mysterious process, about which not everything is known. This is no place to attempt to describe the process in all its gorgeous obscurity; in any event only a moderate number of basic propositions are required to explain the figures the Federal Reserve and the markets regularly issue as a guide to general credit conditions.

Start with the proposition that an enormous flow of funds throughout the system lies beyond the *direct control* of the Federal Reserve. This flow is the so-called real saving generated in the course of economic activity and measured in the national accounts. No activity on the part of the Federal Reserve can alter the fact that individuals save, currently at the rate of about $150 billion a year, or that corporations, in an ordinary recent year, experienced a gross saving flow of retained earnings and depreciation amounting to about $300 billion a year. These flows would persist and, in ordinary times, would find appropriate investment outlets, altogether apart from the activities of the Federal Reserve System.

The Federal Reserve is concerned with the institutional structure of a financial system capable of engaging in the *creation* of credit. This structure comprises the so-called financial intermediaries, of which the typical and far and away the most important is our good friend the commercial bank. It is the great virtue (and at times the great danger) of the commercial banking system that it ordinarily extends an aggregate amount of credit approximately equal to twenty times its own capital. (Some bankers would argue, not without merit, that a well-run bank really requires no capital at all.) The principal function of the Federal Reserve is to regulate the rate of credit creation in the banking system, which can be thought of as the womb of the money supply. No other arm of government can truly create credit; no budget deficits, no lending programs, do anything more than create and augment the demand for credit, and alter the direction of credit flows; they do not add to the supply of credit. The Fed reigns over credit availability and hence has much to say about the cost of credit—that is, interest rates.

Credit creation occurs at the imposing desk of a steely-eyed banker when he reluctantly accepts the loan instrument of a borrower and creates a bank deposit (a liability of the bank) in return for the debt instrument. The deposit liabilities of the commercial banking system are thus the basic reservoir of money and the place where it is created. The control of this process amounts to a control, exercised by the Federal Reserve, over the banks' ability to *lend* (the term used in connection with business and consumer loans) and *invest* (the term used in connection with acquisitions of federal, state, and local securities). The control is exercised through the Federal Reserve's application of a *reserve requirement,* by which banks are required to keep at the Federal Reserve a deposit equal to a certain percentage of their deposit liabilities—amounting to roughly one-sixth of the demand-type liabilities, and about 5 percent of the time-deposit-type liabilities.

In the old days, the distinction between demand deposits and time deposits was precise and simple. Commercial banks were essentially depositary institutions, accepting demand deposits on a non-interest-bearing basis, and accepting time deposits at an interest rate fixed by the Federal Reserve. Massive and rapid deregulation of financial markets generally has produced a proliferation of forms of bank liabilities lying somewhere between demand deposits and time deposits, and banks compete vigorously for varieties of interest-bearing deposits.

In fact, it is no longer really appropriate to call banks depositary institutions; they are aggressive seekers of money in certificates of deposit, in NOW accounts, and in a variety of liquid investment accounts that compete with money-market mutual funds. The Federal Reserve engages in the necessary but somewhat arbitrary process of classifying all these types of accounts, in order to calculate the appropriate reserve requirements against them. Since time deposits are subject to a much lower reserve requirement than demand deposits, the average reserve requirement against the typical commercial bank's deposit liabilities has declined from the high requirement against demand deposits toward the lower requirement against time deposits.

Now for a monstrously oversimplified description of the machinery of Federal Reserve control. The Federal Reserve controls the reserves on deposit from commercial banks, by *open-market activity.* If it wishes to *expand* the reserves of the banking system, it buys government securities in the open market, ultimately paying for them by *crediting* the reserve position of a commercial bank. The consequence is to put the commercial banks further into an open-to-lend reserve position. If it wishes to *shrink* reserves, it sells government securities on the open market and accepts payment in the form of a debit to the reserve position of a commercial bank. This is an ongoing, continuing process; the Federal Reserve is in the market every day.

The Fed can also achieve the same effects of expansion or constraint on bank reserves (and hence on their ability to lend) by altering the percentage reserve requirements against deposits; it has the power to alter these requirements, within ranges set by legislation. A reduction of reserve requirements will free banks to lend more; a rise in reserve requirements will eventually necessitate a contraction of lending.

Finally, the Federal Reserve can make the available credit somewhat more expensive or somewhat cheaper through another device that tends to affect the price of credit. The lending capacity of individual banks is a function of their deposits at the Federal Reserve, and the Federal Reserve stands ready to lend reserves to commercial banks seeking to expand their lending beyond the limit of their own reserve position. Reserves so acquired by a commercial bank are called **borrowed reserves**, (as distinguished from owned or nonborrowed reserves); the borrowing is from the Federal Reserve, at an interest rate called the **discount rate**. When the Fed lowers the discount rate, it is reducing the banks' cost of borrowed reserves.

Alternatively, banks in search of a higher reserve position can borrow reserves from other banks blessed with an excess reserve position. There is thus a kind of market in reserves—a *federal funds* market; the interest rate charged by one bank to lend reserves to another bank is known as the **federal funds rate**, or, more familiarly, the Fed funds rate. Since borrowing reserves from the Fed and borrowing reserves from other banks are alternatives, the discount rate and the Fed funds rate are competitively related. Normally, the discount rate is modestly lower than the Fed funds rate.

The Condition of Financial Markets

Bearing in mind this simple little edifice of law and custom, it is now possible to take a hard look at the statistics by which all this frantic financial activity can be observed. The deposit liabilities of the banking system; the reserve requirement against those liabilities; the surplus or deficit of the commercial banks' actual reserve, relative to the reserve requirement; the borrowings of commercial banks from the Federal Reserve to meet the reserve requirement; and the outstanding loans and investments of the commercial banking system are all published monthly by the Federal Reserve, and even weekly for an aggregation of large money-center commercial banks (whose behavior is not generally typical of all commercial banks). Changes in the Federal Reserve's discount rate are announced immediately (being an administered rate, and not a market rate, it goes for months, and sometimes for years, without change). The federal funds rate, which for obvious reasons is taken to be an important indicator of how comfortable the supply of reserves really is, is reported continuously all day, every day. (Figure 5–4 shows its behavior in recent years, along with that of the discount rate.) A rise in the federal funds rate is generally taken to mean that bank reserve positions have grown more constrictive, the supply of Fed funds has grown scarcer, and the bidding for them by needy borrowers has grown more intense. Since the actual state of reserves is largely controlled by the Fed, movement in the Fed funds rate is an indicator of the mood and intentions of that very important and somewhat secretive institution.

Out of these direct raw materials produced by the ongoing operations of the credit markets, the Federal Reserve derives some fascinating related numbers that are the endless preoccupation of Fed watchers, and of economists in

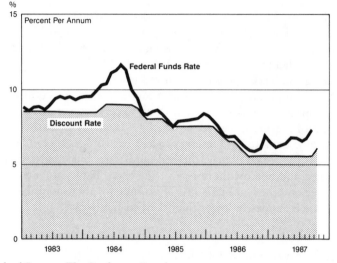

Sources: Federal Reserve; The Conference Board.

Figure 5–4. The Cost of Borrowed Reserves

general. Probably the most watched financial statistic is a mysterious number called the **money supply,** which is very sloppily divided into an M_1 money supply and an M_2 money supply (and then an M_3 money supply, and on and on beyond that, even unto L, for all liquid assets). This classification is a series of nesting boxes: M_1, inside M_2, inside M_3, and so on. The object of this elaborate classification system is to establish definitions of, and then to measure continuously, the supply of money in the system.

There is no easy or handy single definition of *money;* the definitional puzzle has resounded through professional economics ever since it began. Common sense says that *money* is totally liquid, totally negotiable, universally acceptable at face value (although inflation might reduce its real value). The more closely an instrument approximates all these criteria, the more nearly it is money. A ten-dollar bill fits all the requirements, as does a demand deposit—almost. Travelers' checks meet *almost* all the requirements very well, but their negotiability rests on the reputation of the issuer. Checkable deposits that earn interest, as in the case of bank NOW accounts, fit the definition with only a minor delinquency. Such liquid assets are so nearly money as to constitute funds immediately available for spending. In the language of monetary economists, they are *transactions balances* and their supply is considered to have an immediate relevance for present and prospective spending in the economic system. These components, taken together, constitute M_1, the category that fits most tightly the term *money.*

The biggest single component of M_1 is the demand deposits of banks; but

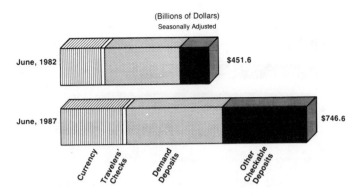

(Billions of Dollars)
Seasonally Adjusted

June, 1982 — $451.6

June, 1987 — $746.6

Currency | Travelers' Checks | Demand Deposits | Other Checkable Deposits

Sources: Federal Reserve; The Conference Board.

Figure 5–5. The Composition of M_1 Money Stock

currency outstanding is about three-fifths as big as demand deposits, and the so-called other checkable deposits are now more than half as big as the demand deposits. Taken together, M_1, at this writing, is about $750 billion. Figure 5–5 shows the composition of M_1 in mid-1987. The Federal Reserve has until recently sought to control this aggregate and set targets for its proposed growth, because very rapid growth would seem to suggest a powerful impending surge in demand and hence an inflationary consequence for the economy as a whole. The Fed's equipment—particularly the open-market activity that controls bank lending and hence the open-to-lend position of the banks reflected in demand deposits—has been directed toward this principal objective.

A second class of money, conveniently described as M_2, includes all of M_1 but also what might be called some secondary reserves of money, in the form of smaller time deposits (under $100,000) at commercial banks and at thrift institutions, and funds in the hands of money-market mutual funds. This somewhat broader measure loses the immediacy of its contact with the economic system, because the additional components are thought to have, in some degree, the character of *saving,* rather than a supply of funds intended for prompt spending.

Finally, to M_2 are added large time deposits (over $100,000) and the money-market deposits of institutions (also generally large amounts), which are considered to have primarily interest-rate and yield objectives, thus departing still further from a transaction balance. The astute reader will have guessed that this classification is called M_3. Finally, there are a host of other financial instruments—including, among others, savings bonds, short-term Treasury securities, bankers acceptances, and commercial paper—that are near money in many respects but more distant in others. Nevertheless, they

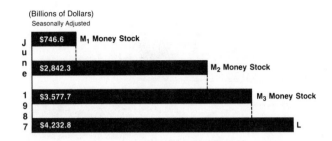

(Billions of Dollars)
Seasonally Adjusted

Sources: Federal Reserve; The Conference Board.

Figure 5–6. Definition of the Money Stock

are taken to represent forms of liquidity and are therefore added to M_3 to produce the ultimate measure of liquid financial assets in the system, known as L. Figure 5–6 shows the relative sizes of these various money measures.

More recently, the behavior of M_1 has seemed to suggest that it has become far less relevant, both to the growth of demand in the economic system as a whole, and to the outlook for inflation. Some of the components of M_1 grew at a spectacular rate in 1986, with little visible consequences for the system. It is widely (and very credibly) argued that the growth of M_1 was a reflection of a general decline in all interest rates, and that as the rates declined the incentive to move funds out of M_1 into other financial assets was reduced. In other words, the character of M_1 as purely necessary transaction balances was compromised by the deregulation that permitted much of M_1 to earn interest, and then by the reduction of the spread in yields between what could be earned in M_1 forms and what was available outside M_1.

As a result of these conditions, at least in part, the money statistics began to develop another gross peculiarity. If the money stock is thought of as the supply of funds entering into the transactions included in GNP, then the ratio of the GNP to the money stock becomes a kind of "turnover" rate for the money stock, or (in the turnover term typically used in this connection) a measure of the "velocity" of money. Almost throughout the postwar years, M_1 experienced a gradual increase in velocity, of perhaps 2.5 percent per year, reflecting generally rising interest rates and hence more efficient use of the money (faster collections through computerization). The uptrend of velocity was taken to be a basic and dependable component of the money function—until 1982, when the velocity trend was suddenly broken by the rate decline (see figure 5–7). The velocity rose again briefly, and then entered on a renewed decline in 1986. It has apparently risen again in 1987; but it is still substantially lower than it was six years ago. The interruption of the uptrend in M_1 velocity doubtless reflects the change in the definition of M_1, again because it incorporates interest-bearing accounts in the total. But the

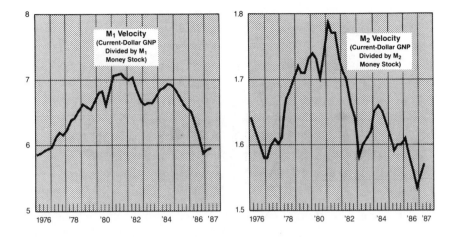

Sources: Federal Reserve; The Conference Board.

Figure 5–7. The Subsidence of Money Velocity

velocities of M_2 and even M_3, which have not been importantly altered definitionally, appear to have fallen considerably over the past several years.

Money accordingly seems abundantly available, perhaps even excessively available, given the needs of the slowly growing real economy of the past several years. But the abundance of liquidity, over and above the apparent needs of the real world, seems to have conduced to a fantastic explosion of activity in the financial world (financial transactions in existing assets are not, of course, real output and are therefore not included in the GNP). In any event, the enormous multiplication of transaction values in financial markets over the past several years likewise suggests that there is abundant credit available for the real world, when it should call for it; and in turn this suggests that the existing stock of money is not now a hindrance to fast growth in the system, and that it might even be adequate to support a rising rate of inflation. For these reasons, the new chairman of the Federal Reserve, Alan Greenspan, appears to subscribe very fully to the views of his distinguished predecessor, Paul Volcker, in considering inflation still to be an important threat to U.S. economic stability.

The classification of M_1, running to L, is built on the measurement of financial assets. For every financial asset there is, of course, a financial debt. (For some debts—long-term debts of governments, corporate-bond indebtedness, indebtedness on mortgages—the financial instrument that constitutes the asset is so long-term and so open to fluctuation in the course of its existence that it is not considered to be *money* at all.) In recent years,

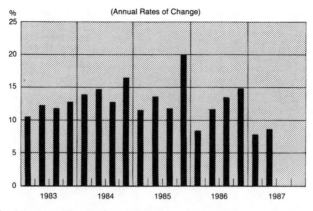

Sources: Federal Reserve; The Conference Board.

Figure 5–8. Debt of Domestic Nonfinancial Sectors

the Federal Reserve has accordingly constructed a debt aggregate that covers the obligations (as distinguished from the assets) of all domestic nonfinancial sectors, including all loans of government. The rate of growth of this aggregate debt figure is of intense interest itself; its components are reported in considerable detail in the quarterly Federal Reserve publication called "Flow of Funds," but monthly estimates are published by the Federal Reserve. Figure 5–8 shows the growth rate of this debt aggregate in recent years.

All these measures of money constitute a definition of *money* from its narrowest to its broadest conception. All the definitions are of significance to the Federal Reserve and to the financial markets, and therefore to business-persons and investors.

Although the Federal Reserve's control over this structure is heavily concentrated in the components that directly involve the extension of bank credit, its influence radiates across all the other categories, for a powerful and important reason. The interest rates available throughout the entire range of securities are tied together by the inevitable arbitrage among them. If the Federal Reserve uses its power to make bank reserves less available, the inevitable consequence is higher interest rates in short-term securities markets. Such higher short-term rates compete with all other forms in which liquidity can be carried; hence they drive up yields in parts of the structure not directly controlled by the Federal Reserve, as the whole structure seeks a competitive equilibrium. In general, the interest rates throughout this structure tend to move together, although normally short-term rates move faster and farther than long-term rates, and there are even periods (such as the summer of 1984) in which other influences playing exclusively on segments of the whole structure can produce a pattern of cross-trends. (In the summer of 1984, short-term rates rose because business was strong, demand for credit was

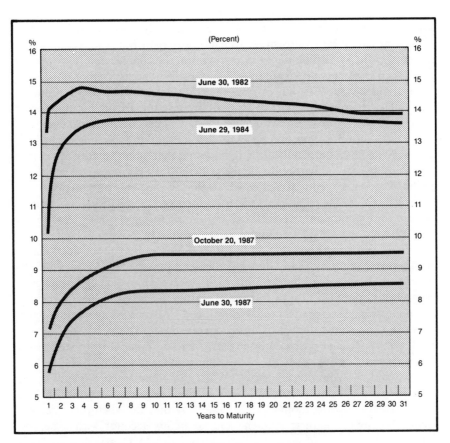

Sources: U.S. Department of the Treasury; The Conference Board.

Figure 5-9. The Yield Curve of Treasury Securities

relatively strong, and the Federal Reserve was relatively restrictive; at the same time, a dwindling of fears of inflation—the *bête noir* of long-term investors—produced a strengthening of bond prices and a decline in long-term yields.) The interest rates that have prevailed among various parts of the money spectrum are seen in figure 5-9, which shows the *yield curve* of Treasury securities at four points in time.

Now some final words on the integration of these two immensely powerful economic instruments in the hands of the federal government. An earlier section treated a large federal budget deficit as stimulative, in a first-round analysis. It is stimulative because the federal government issues risk-free securities to obtain its necessary increment of cash, and then spends the cash, leaving the rest of the system with all the cash it had in the first place plus an increment of risk-free securities that are very nearly cash in the eyes of the holder. At the moment the government seeks its cash, however, it is competing for the attention of investors, to capture part of the real saving that is going on in the system all the time; if it wins in the competition (as it always does, of course), it is depriving the private sector of access to that portion of the ongoing saving. It is thus tapping the *real* saving of the system, reducing the availabilities to other borrowers, and presumably driving up the interest rates the other borrowers will have to pay. The consequence does not increase the money supply and poses no threat of inflation as long as the government's needs are met out of the real saving; that would simply mean that the government would grow, while the growth of the private sector would be inhibited by lesser credit, at higher rates—that is, the private sector would be "crowded out" of the credit markets. If business were in recession at the time, its need for credit might be very low, and the financing of the federal deficit would have no consequences not already imposed by recession itself.

However—a big however—in an effort to accommodate the demands of the Treasury, there are many things the Federal Reserve can do. It can make banks very open to lend by elevating their reserves, in which case the banks themselves could buy a lot of the new Treasury securities, relieving the private nonfinancial sector of a need to do so, and forestalling any rise in interest rates. The Fed would do this by direct open-market activity, buying some of the Treasury securities itself. A large part—perhaps even all—of the issues of Treasury securities to cover the debt could thus be placed with the Federal Reserve and the commercial banks. When the commercial banks buy the securities, they pay for them by crediting the Treasury's accounts; in this sense they are creating money in the same way they do when they accept a private borrower's loan instrument and credit his account with a deposit liability. The result, of course, is to expand the M measures of money, through creation of credit.

This process—often called *monetization of debt*—is generally considered temporarily desirable (certainly at least excusable) in the course of a recession, when the whole system is underemployed and increases in credit for both government and the private sector appear to be desirable stimuli. But when the private sector is doing very well, thank you, and is urgently seeking credit for its own expansive views of its future, the Federal Reserve is naturally less inclined to add fuel to what may in the end be an inflationary fire. If it does not accommodate the borrowing requirements of the Treasury to finance the deficit, it will force the financing onto the private sector at a time when the private sector has a lot of its own financing to do. The aggregate **demand for credit**—the debt variable that the Federal Reserve watches— would grow rapidly if the Federal Reserve were to be accommodative under such circumstances; if it is not accommodative, the federal borrowing needs will compete, occasionally violently, with the borrowing needs of the private sector, and the whole structure of interest rates will rise. Since the federal government borrows when it needs to, regardless of interest rates, in the end it will be the private sector that will be priced out. Those demands in the private sector that are heavily dependent on credit—purchases of major consumer durables, purchases of plant and equipment, and housing construction in particular—will suffer. The inventory policies of business will grow more conservative on account of the high interest cost of carrying the inventory.

A big budget deficit is thus stimulative to the economy *only* if it is accommodated by monetary policy—that is, *only* if the Federal Reserve will meet the demand of the deficit as well as the aggregate private demand. It is *not* stimulative, if the Federal Reserve refuses to accommodate the demand. A big deficit and a restrictive, nonaccommodative monetary policy are thus operating in conflict; indeed, they operated in just such conflict throughout the early 1980s, when outcomes for interest rates and for economic activity were extremely cyclical and destabilizing.

Such dramatic conflicts in the applications of economic policy often have substantial side-effect consequences, and the consequences are often difficult to foresee. In the early 1980s, the enormous appetite of the federal government for credit was an invitation to capital all over the world. The road to investment in the United States inevitably ran headlong through the market for the dollar, raising it far above its value as measured in conventional purchasing-power terms, and the merchandise trade position of the United States, where it precipitated a flood of imports. Further description of this machinery is reserved for chapter 6; but here it might be noted that the huge surge of imported goods into the United States that reflected the high dollar also suppressed American inflation, with the peculiar and unpredictable result that a huge deficit in the federal budget occurred in the presence of a major decline in the inflation rate.

The conflicted, irresolute, theoretically paradoxical condition that has beset economic policy in the 1980s, is thus not an accident, and it does not simply reflect bureaucratic stupidity. The budget deficit that exists today, and seems to impend for the next several years, in part reflects decisions of government to enhance U.S. incentives to work and invest through reduction of tax rates. The Federal Reserve, on the other hand, accepts its commitment to provide credit for the growth of the economy; but it is acutely aware of the proposition, accepted by almost all economists, that very rapid growth of money—faster than the probable growth rate of real activity in the economy—threatens to bid up prices and turn the system toward a high and destructive general inflation. The joint target of the two arms of policy can be said to be a vigorously growing economy, with considerable new investment for efficiency and growth in the future, a relatively low level of unemployment, and relatively stable prices. Economic outcomes are very hard to predict, however, and events not controlled by either of the two arms of policy often intervene to upset even the most careful calculations and to drive the system away from one or several of the agreed target conditions. Doubtless the federal government—the administration and the Congress as well—would be eager to seek a lower budget deficit, requiring less financing; the Federal Reserve would doubtless prefer to see lower interest rates, and probably less aggregate debt formation. The figures charted in this chapter, on the condition of the federal budget and federal debt, and on the money stock and the rate of growth of debt, frame an unresolved issue for the rest of the decade.

6
The United States in the World

The United States is far and away the world's largest national economy. Its geographical size, and its wide range of climate and of soils, together with its isolation from the rest of the developed world, have throughout its history made it a uniquely independent nation, requiring little from others. The huge size and rapid growth of its domestic market have provided ample opportunity to its native industries. Its open border with Canada, and its partly common heritage, have for a century produced substantial volumes of trade with its northern neighbor; as for the rest, the United States historically has had almost the smallest international sector of any of the developed economies.

This high degree of independence, bordering on economic isolation, has been fundamentally altered in the postwar years, to the point where it is no longer really possible to understand U.S. economic experience without reference to its large and growing—and now very troubled—linkages with the rest of the world. Chapter 1 reviewed the progressive involution of the U.S. international position, as an element in the long history of its postwar wave of growth and subsidence. In any event, the trade flows, the investment flows, and the financial and currency flows that tie the United States to its trading partners are now of such dramatic importance that they exert large influences on even the most determinedly domestic business operations in the United States.

International economics, a highly developed specialty within the general field, has many complicated things to say about the nature of international markets and the international consequences of domestic economic policies. In this area, the disputes among the specialists are particularly intense, running even to the very nature of international economic adjustment.

In general, theory views the international market as a discipline on the performance of individual economies; to put it as simply as possible, highly stimulative misbehavior at home, in the unwise political pursuit of domestic happiness, will be judged and punished in the world market. The eating of domestic substance shrinks exports, draws in imports, and reduces the value of the currency relative to other currencies because it grows so abundant abroad in payment for the excess of imports. The decline of the currency elevates the cost of imports and contributes an international component to the inflation that domestic misbehavior would cause in any event. In the hoary days of the gold standard, substantial international deficits drew down the nation's gold supply, shrinking the base of its currency, threatening credit stringency and serious recession. In free-market international theory, crime (improvident behavior at home) still begets punishment (inflation if the currency weakens, recession if imported goods flood the domestic market, and falling living standards).

Simply put, this is the great retributive mechanism of international economics. The United States has been a dominant and powerful economy in the world for a long time; and the respect accorded to it (and to its currency), as well as its near self-sufficiency in almost everything, and its technological lead, have for much of its history freed it from the iron laws of international economics. But as chapter 1 pointed out at length, the circumstances on which this proud isolation was based have now very largely disappeared. Advanced technology has been spread all around the world (in part by the foreign investment of U.S. companies), where it is often combined with labor costs far lower than our own. The U.S. dollar, formerly held in enormously high regard, is nevertheless no longer convertible into gold as it was during the twenty-five years of the gold-exchange standard developed at Bretton Woods; and its value, relative to other currencies, declined dramatically from early 1985 into late 1987. The United States is a substantial exporter of both agricultural goods and manufactured goods; but it is now also the world's biggest importer, and its imports, even of manufactured goods, far exceed its exports. In 1984 pressures to protect domestic markets from further inroads of imports besieged the Congress and the administration. Huge volumes of dollars exist in the world markets—the residues of prolonged payments deficits and of the successful recycling of the petrodollars earned by the Organization of Petroleum Exporting Countries (OPEC) in the years of its dominance over the world's oil markets. By 1987, the United States had become the biggest net debtor in the world, as it settled its bumper-size trade deficits in dollars—dollars that represent claims on U.S. output.

For the United States, this is a new, tough ball game, its risks compounded by the virtually total internationalization of financial markets (with their capacity for gigantic volumes of financial transfers at electronic speed), and further compounded by the extreme volumes of lending to developed countries engaged in by major U.S. banks with substantial international operations. The risks in our international accounts are now too big to be ignored by any U.S. industry, however isolated it may be from direct international competition.

The basic concept in the measurement of international economic relations, similar in some ways to the national accounts for domestic economics, is called the **balance of payments**—an aggregate measure of the flows of goods and services between the United States and its multiple trading partners. The form of this accounting system has changed over the years as the international currency arrangements have changed. In today's world of floating currencies detached from gold, attention focuses most particularly on what is called the *current account,* whose surplus or deficit is inevitably settled in dollars.

The current account records all international sales—of services as well as goods—between the United States and its trading partners. Its principal components are merchandise exports and imports (the difference is called the *trade balance*); tourism outlay of U.S. travelers abroad, less the outlays of foreign travelers in the United States; and the investment income earned by U.S. investment abroad, less the investment earnings of others on their investment in the United States. Only the merchandise trade portion of the account is available monthly; the whole account is prepared quarterly by the U.S. Department of Commerce.

The net-exports line in the gross national product, which is the national-accounts reflection of much of this activity, is approximately the equivalent of the current account. The major components of the current account are shown in figure 6–1, which reveals an enormous descent into deficit on the part of the **U.S. merchandise balance,** and a partially offsetting surplus on the so-called *invisibles*—the nontrade tourism and investment flows.

The merchandise trade pattern shown in figure 6–1 is the ultimate reflection of several conditions. The present deficit illustrates all of them. In the first place, since 1983 the United States has been experiencing a faster expansion in aggregate domestic demand than has appeared among any of its trading partners; our market for the exports of others has grown much faster than their market for our exports. Second, the immense recovery in the exchange value of the dollar from 1980 to early 1985 meant that foreign products appeared to be relatively cheap (even though their prices were rising in terms of their own domestic currencies, the dollar commanded much more of their currencies). Conversely, the high dollar meant that it took much more foreign currency to buy U.S. products. Our exports were thus shrunken by their higher costs, while imports were stimulated by their lower cost.

The spread of advanced technology, even into developing countries where labor costs are dramatically lower than in the United States (and where the domestic propensity to consume is very low), has created a whole new range of low-cost competitive products. Finally—and, as history may write, perhaps most important—the Pacific Basin (Japan, South Korea, Taiwan, Hong Kong, Singapore) has witnessed an explosion of output among countries with spectacularly low propensities for domestic consumption. This powerful independent reason for the U.S. trade dilemma, of course, augments all the other reasons for a trade deficit.

Given the enormous supply of dollars already existing around the world,

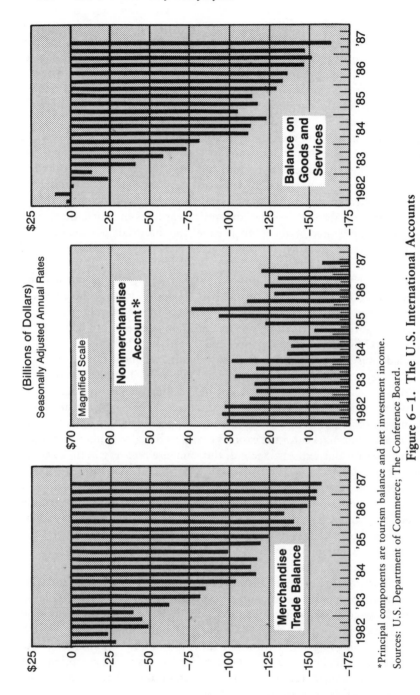

Figure 6–1. The U.S. International Accounts

*Principal components are tourism balance and net investment income.

Sources: U.S. Department of Commerce; The Conference Board.

and the increment to the supply that results from our settlement of our current-account deficit, one would expect (that is, international economic theory would argue) that the U.S. dollar should have been weak, not strong, in 1984. Figure 6–2 reveals how phenomenally strong it was. Not everything is known about why it was so strong, but at least some of the reasons are clear. With a burgeoning recovery that required a lot of credit to sustain it, with a very large budget deficit requiring financing, and with a Federal Reserve that remained studiously alert to any excesses in the provision of created credit, U.S. interest rates were strikingly high in the first half of the 1980s. The high interest rates available in the United States made dollar investments here particularly attractive, and the demand for dollars for this purpose were enormous. The outflow of dollars resulting from the need to settle our international deficits seemed to make a quick U-turn, returning to our own shores for investment at interest rates that exceed those available in most of the rest of the world. This investment opportunity was reinforced in 1984 by the prevailing view that the dollar is a safe currency—a haven against the political and economic vicissitudes that may well beset less vigorous or less stable economies and their currencies. The huge dollar-exchange

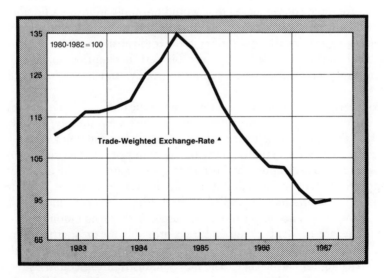

▲ Based on pre-June 1970 parities.

Sources: Morgan Guaranty Trust Company; The Conference Board.

Figure 6–2. The Course of the Dollar

market—doubtless by a vast multiple the biggest market in the world, and almost totally unsupervised—thus had a wonderful product, among the safest currencies anywhere and among the highest-yielding investments. Thus the outflow of dollars returns as an inflow—now, of course, owned by nationals of other countries. (This is the common form of the statement. The impression it conveys is not wrong; but in actuality, the dollars involved never leave the United States. Instead, the ownership of the dollars changes hands, from a U.S. national to a foreign holder.)

The accumulating reinvestment of foreign-owned dollars in the United States has been so massive that it has eroded the U.S. net investment position throughout the world; and the surplus the United States has always earned on its net investment abroad is certainly deteriorating under present conditions, accentuating the total deterioration in the current account. The deterioration of the current account necessarily implies a still greater outflow of dollars.

This international dilemma is traceable to a set of sequential anomalies in the U.S. economic situation in the years 1981 to 1985: a very high budget deficit conducive to very high interest rates, which in turn are conducive to a very high dollar, which in turn is conducive to a substantial trade deficit. The payment remains in the United States, attracted by the high interest rates, and as a form of saving helps in some degree to finance the budget deficit that stands at the beginning of this train of consequences. The dollar exchange value in 1984 was, by general agreement, far too high on a purchasing-power basis; the evidence for that conclusion is the trade deficit itself. But the international economic consequences that would normally follow—a flooding of the world with unwanted dollars, hence a decline in the value of the dollar, and hence a return toward equilibrium in the trade position—were forestalled by the combination of loose fiscal policy (big deficits requiring financing) and firm monetary policy (restricted supply of credit, and hence high interest rates).

From early 1985 far into 1987, the value of the dollar, relative to the currencies of other major developed economies, fell very sharply indeed. By mid-1987, the currency adjustment had progressed to the point where U.S. production costs were actually lower in many industries than they were in Germany and Japan. Exports had begun to grow again, and the importation rate appeared to have stabilized. But the issue is far from resolved. Some markets for U.S. exports have dwindled, in more than a short-term sense. The OPEC countries can no longer buy U.S. output with the abandon they could afford in the late 1970s. U.S. agriculture is probably the most efficient in the world, but other countries that were major importers of U.S. farm products are approaching self-sufficiency. The newly industrializing countries (South Korea, Taiwan, Hong Kong, and Singapore, among others) address themselves to U.S. markets (the most attractive, of course, in the world) equipped with state-of-the-art-technology and far lower labor costs. Finally, the United

States has emerged into a high-consumption, low-saving phase of its history; perhaps its saddest current statistics are the continuing high rate of importation of other countries' savings and the application of these savings to consumption purposes in the United States.

The United States has opportunities to escape from this consumption millstone by tax increases and monetary conditions that militate against spending and elevate the reward for saving. But it seems probable, as this is written, that a failure of U.S. policy to pursue these directions will simply mean that the rest of the world, now massive holders of our currency, will impose the conditions on us through higher inflation, and higher interest rates, both of which constrain domestic consumption and living standards.

For the U.S. businessperson, whether heavily involved in international trade or not, these considerations pose one of the great issues of the late 1980s. They clearly are among the root causes of the collapse of the U.S. equity market in late 1987. The failure of economic policy to come to grips with them militates against any casual optimism about the U.S. economic outlook in the rest of this decade.

7
Inflation and Economic Policies

Along with unemployment (which in many respects is its obverse manifestation), inflation is one of the great enemies of a market economy. Inflation, actual or anticipated, is a mover of business judgment, a powerful influence on consumer attitudes, a displacer of our international position, a major influence on economic policy. An understanding of it is essential to reasoned appraisal of the U.S. outlook. Understanding it isn't easy, however.

As with any other important variable in a complex structure, the rate of inflation is both a consequence of and a causal influence on the behavior of the system as a whole. Changes in the inflation rate, for whatever reason, have significant effects on aggregate economic performance; they also have important distributive effects, altering the fortunes of debtors and creditors, and producing differential consequences as between importers and exporters, consumption industries and investment industries, and holders of goods and holders of financial instruments.

These differential consequences make inflation a contentious political subject—all the more so since the causes of changes in the inflation rate are themselves a matter of dispute. Embedded as it is in a broad range of intense self-interest issues close to the hearts of various segments of the electorate, inflation in its elevated phases becomes a center of political and even philosophical debate that occasionally approaches religious intensity, clouding its real significance for business. In the early 1970s and again in the late 1970s, inflation control became the overriding criterion of policy, superseding job creation, growth, and cyclical stability.

By virtue of their supposed consequences for inflation, the two principal instruments of economic policy—the management of money and credit, and the management of the federal budget—acquire powerful emotive significance that is played on, often in an alarmist way, in the political process. Fiscal policies and monetary policies, however, affect much more than just the inflation rate; they influence employment, economic growth, credit availability to consumers and investors, the services provided by government, and the burden of government costs resting on the private sector. To understand the U.S. price environment and to grasp its future, it seems essential that we seek a practical, nondoctrinal appraisal of the record in the United States, and of the causes that have led to the consequences, if we are to arrive at realistic and sustainable relationships between the inflation rate and the many other criteria by which our economic performance is judged.

We should first recognize that the character of inflation changes as the rate rises. The difference between the inflation rate experienced in the 1970s and the 2 percent average rate experienced in the 1950s is not simply a matter of numbers; it is profoundly qualitative. At some point between the two experiences, inflation changes its character so dramatically as to invite altogether different appraisal—even, one might think, a different name. A high rate of inflation colors the real world with expectational speculative incentives that distort behavior and sap real activity by diverting attention to balance-sheet concerns. Investment decisions acquire complex new dimensions, and incentives to save deteriorate. The capricious and inequitable distribution of the burden of inflation intensifies the distributive struggle over shares of output, and the search for parochial shelter from inflation accentuates the general rate. An elevated rate of inflation also tends to generate a stream of policy decisions and institutional adjustments that are not necessarily desirable on other grounds and may, in fact, be self-defeating.

Inflation is not, in itself, subject to ethical characterization; it is not inherently good or bad. The rate is undesirably high when adverse economic consequences can be shown to ensue, or to be probable. An inflation rate *not* accompanied by (or threatening to produce) such consequences may not be theoretically beautiful, but its treatment should take account of the many other criteria by which economic performance should be judged—particularly the criteria of job creation, living standards, and the rate of private investment.

Economic policy can certainly accelerate inflation. One need not subscribe to doctrinal monetarism to agree that there are rates of creation of money and credit so substantially faster than the growth of actual and potential output as to be conducive to a too-high aggregate and general rate of inflation, at least for a time. One need not be religious about the desirability of balancing the federal budget to accept the conclusion that large and prolonged federal deficits complicate life for a central bank charged with the responsibility for avoiding high inflation; in the end, its alternatives become financing an undesirable rate of inflation, or driving interest rates to levels that will depress the private economy as a whole, and its investment function in particular. Ultimately, economic policy is made by our elected representatives—the administration and the Congress. Even a supposedly independent central bank has no real mandate to maintain an anti-inflation posture beyond the point where the interest-rate consequences for economic performance become violently depressive, as measured by unemployment, living standards and investment rates. Budget deficits are too high, and ultimately inflationary, when they impose these alternatives on the central bank.

Although policy can cause inflation, the historical record of monetary policy and fiscal policy in the United States displays a considerable conservative sensitivity to the threat of inflation. The actual record of the growth of credit in the United States—and, until recently, the actual record of federal deficits—by no means suggest improvident policymaking. Nor does the record of the inflation rate itself in the United States suggest a persistent or systematic loss of control over the U.S. price level. The record in the United States lends little support to the conclusion that we have brought inflation on ourselves by persistent policy mistakes.

The long history of the money stock in the United States, relative to the aggregate gross national product (all expressed in current dollars) hardly suggests a clear causal relationship to inflation. Most measures of money and credit availability appear to have grown modestly over the long term, and less rapidly than the GNP itself. The volume of M_1 is far below the relative levels of ten or fifteen years ago. In fact, if M_1 were to be adjusted by the inflation rate itself, its real volume still appeared no higher, until recently, than fifteen years ago. (Figure 7–1 shows the long history of the money stock, in current dollars, and deflated by a price index to indicate changes in its purchasing power.)

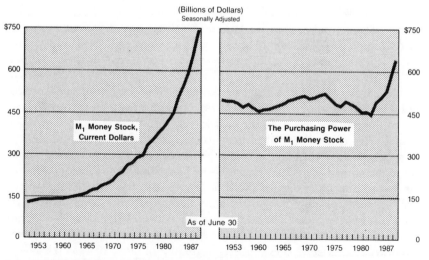

Sources: Federal Reserve; The Conference Board.

Figure 7–1. The Narrow (M_1) Money Stock

It is true that waves in the growth rate of money are correlated with ensuing waves in price statistics—a point on which monetarists rest their statistical case. The availability of credit, however, is an influence not just on the price level but on the volume of real activity as well. Simple correlation of money growth with inflation overflies the normal sequence of causality that any businessperson will recognize—the trail runs from money, to real markets, to strained resources, to prices. The cyclical rise and fall in the strength of markets should certainly be given some weight in explanation of price behavior. In its periodic ventures into relatively rapid money growth (as, for example, in the last half of 1982), the Federal Reserve has generally reacted to the legitimate and understandable need to improve economic performance as measured by such real criteria as the unemployment rate and the trend of real investment.

In any event, the issue is not whether money *can* cause inflation (of course it can), but whether the management of credit in the United States has been such as to identify it as a clear, substantial, and independent cause of the inflation itself. The record does not support such an argument.

Much the same point might be made for federal budgets and federal deficits. Until recently, most of the deficits experienced since World War II were very largely explained by the response of revenues to the business cycle; the structural, active, noncyclical component of the deficits has generally been small. The structural portion of the deficit has often been in surplus in the past twenty years, even as recently as early 1981. The relationship of the federal debt (viewed as the accumulation of past and ongoing deficits) to aggregate GNP, as shown in figure 7–2, subsided from nearly 1.0 in the early years to under 0.35 in the late 1970s (it has been rising sharply in the early 1980s). Again, the issue is not whether deficits *can* cause inflation, but whether the *actual* deficits have been such as to constitute a clear, substantial, and independent cause. Again, the long historical record does not support such an argument.

Indeed, the postwar history of inflation itself in the United States carries the same suggestion of moderate behavior, certainly for the first quarter century of the postwar years. In the past fifteen years, the U.S. price level has certainly experienced several serious accelerations of inflation, but they do not appear to have been related to any permanent bias of policy toward inflation in the United States (see figure 7–3). In the late 1960s the buildup of a war that so hopelessly divided the U.S. people as to forestall and delay ordinary financing, produced a kind of guns-and-butter crisis, with inflationary potentials; but the potentials were contained by two comparatively moderate surges of interest rates tolerated by the Federal Reserve, and ultimately by a temporary tax. A second escalation, beginning in late 1972 (as the Nixon incomes-policy effort was gradually abandoned) and continuing through 1973, appears to have been at least partly related to a general coincidence of

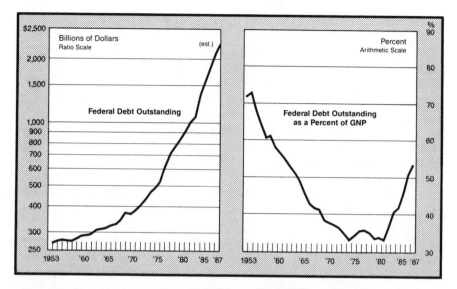

Sources: U.S. Department of the Treasury; The Conference Book.

Figure 7–2. The Federal Debt and Its Relationship to GNP

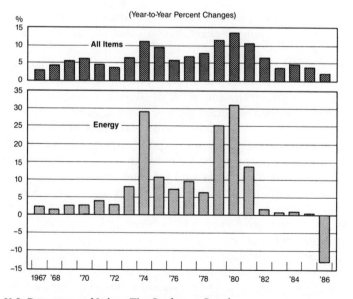

Sources: U.S. Department of Labor; The Conference Board.

Figure 7–3. Consumer Prices and the Explosion in Energy Prices

business-cycle expansions throughout the West, in the presence of a rapidly developing Eurodollar market that contributed the liquidity for a near doubling of the international commodity price level. This experience was immensely aggravated by an unprecedented elevation of oil prices, and a pronounced rise in agricultural prices because of crop failures. In 1979 another lesser but still dramatic elevation of oil prices, together with another surge in farm prices, restored double-digit inflation.

In all these instances the Federal Reserve appears to have behaved predictably in the exercise of its domestic powers, and thereby to have confronted *international* inflation by curbing the supply of *domestic* credit, elevating interest rates, and producing recession. When international recession followed U.S. domestic recession, the inflation rate was reduced, and the Fed then inevitably turned its attention back to the stimulation of domestic recovery and growth.

Monetarism may argue that if monetary policy were not to have accommodated such surges in the price level in their early stages, they could not have occurred; that is, under a strict monetary regime, the rise in the prices of the directly affected commodities (petroleum products, food) would have been offset by falling prices for other commodities, producing *relative* price change but not *aggregate* inflation. This argument assumes a perfectly fluid equilibrium market system, perfectly mobile resources, and perfectly flexible prices in predominantly auction markets. These assumptions are fatally unrealistic. Much of the extraordinary inflation experience of the 1970s, and much of the instability of interest rates in that decade, is owing not to misbehavior of economic policymakers, but to conditions beyond the reach of policy.

Apart from the behavior of economic policy and of international influences on the price level, there are several other powerful influences at work on the long-term price behavior of all developed economies. These other causes may be described as sociological, structural, institutional changes in the economic system that contribute a structural component to the inflation rate. They are not generally amenable to policy constraint; indeed, the effort to control their consequences through conventional aggregative economic policy may have prohibitive social and economic costs.

The record of inflation in the last two decades is colored by a progressive evolution in economic institutions, and the legislated objectives of the economic system, particularly in the years between 1965 and 1980, which witnessed an elaboration of social compacts in the area of social security, medical insurance, unemployment protection, and welfare programs. This proliferating structure of nonmarket costs is referred to in chapter 1, and is further described in chapter 8. Here it should be noted that the rapid growth of these programs (and others) carries obvious significance for the underlying inflationary tendencies of the system — not simply because they run headlong through the federal budget and account for some of the deficits now being experienced, but also because they deliberately break the free-market bond between risk and reward. The third-party payment systems that prevail across much of these programs inevitably stimulate demand for services (for example, medical services), and lower some of the incentives on which crude economic efficiency rests. They are intended to reach ethical objectives, not economic ones; their cost tends to be distributed in part by inflation.

These reflections on some of the more obvious evolving aspects of the U.S. economy (and of all modern, developed economies) would seem to be essential parts of the understanding of modern inflation; they help to disclose the limits of economic policy when it seeks to confront the inflation issue, and they help to clarify why grimly determined efforts to treat inflation only through conventional restrictive *domestic* policies carry such heavy costs and frequently produce perverse results. The actual prevailing institutional and sociological structure of the system is an integral part of the real world to which economic policy must address itself; that world contains an inflation tendency that inheres in our institutions.

Economists do not like this argument; evolving sociological conditions are hard to quantify, they do not seem to help in forecasting, they tend to escape from presumably scientific theories of the origins of inflation, they seem to somewhat reduce the significance of pure economics, and they suggest limits to its power to direct events. Yet that is precisely where we are. Modern inflation is not simply painted on the real world by errors of economic policy; it is in the grain. If monetary policy is to obliterate *all* evidence of inflation in the system, arising from *all* the multiple causes, it will have to be violent and, periodically, extremely costly, as indeed it has been in several prolonged episodes over the past twenty years.

These reflections on inflation and its causes lead to the following conclusions, useful in appraising the future of the U.S. inflation rate and the policies that will be used to combat inflation.

1. Doctrinal crusades against inflation that rest on a narrow policy-oriented view of its causes cannot be successful, and carry heavy potential cost. Crusading zeal on inflation should be treated circumspectly; the crusade often draws support from parochial objectives.

2. There are rates of inflation that are clearly detrimental to the system as a whole, and to its future. Leaving this issue simply in the hands of the Federal Reserve is logically wrong, impractical in the real world, and occasionally dangerously costly. Conversely, there are targets for inflation rates that are unrealistically and unsustainably low; dedicating policy to such unrealistic objectives over any prolonged period carries heavy real costs. To the extent that inflation is structural and sociological, its home is in the struc-

ture of legislation and custom that dictate nonmarket objectives for the system.

3. The budget deficits that have persisted in much of this decade, and threaten to continue to the end of the decade, are abnormally and dangerously high. They represent a major departure from the federal budget experience of the postwar years, and vastly complicate the efforts of the Federal Reserve to maintain credit conditions compatible with vigorous growth of private business. Left untreated, they must in the end threaten to restore the struggle between monetary policy and fiscal policy that produced the interest rates and deplorable economic experience of mid-1981 to mid-1982. They are not compatible with a system that depends mainly on private incentive for its energy, and on private investment for its growth. Indeed, losses of investment during recessions induced by Federal Reserve struggles with inflation are themselves inflationary, in a longer-term context.

4. Deficits of the immense size experienced in the past several years may have such complex consequences that their inflation potential may be disguised, and deferred into the future. As indicated in chapter 6, the huge deficits of the years since 1982 produced a shortage of real saving in the United States, and required a massive capital inflow for their financing. This inflow from the rest of the world inevitably passed through the market for the dollar, driving up its value, and making foreign goods appear cheap. The sequential result was a rapid rise in imports of goods into the United States, which depressed the markets available for domestic producers, and suppressed the inflation rate throughout the goods sector of the U.S. economy. Inevitably, the dollar has long since passed through a speculative peak, and its immense and rapid decline beginning in early 1985 and continuing at least until late 1987, is reversing the conditions that suppressed inflation. It is altogether expectable, at this writing, that the inflation rate in the remainder of this decade will be higher than might be implied by domestic economic conditions themselves.

5. Since our institutional structure, and the social and political commitments of our economic system, play so significant a role in the inflation rate, efforts to contain this cause are fundamental to the restraint of general inflation. Progress in constraining the inflationary consequences of institutions would relieve the overcommitment of the Federal Reserve to this issue, which often leads it to engage in broad and costly assaults on the measured inflation rate. In pursuit of this objective, the Congress should be made intelligently aware of the fact that although transfer programs may be an essential and desirable response of a democratic political system, they are not free goods; they carry connotations of some degree of inflation, and the acceptance of some degree of recession, or both. The ethical considerations that have led to the enlargement of transfer programs are valid recognitions of a need to ameliorate extremes in the distribution of income, health, education, and opportunity. Their growth, however, inevitably elevates the inflation rate

associated with high employment. The benefits of these programs are in a trade-off relationship with the inefficiencies and costs associated with an elevated inflation rate.

6. Apart from the issue of the treatment of social costs, other mechanisms characteristic of mixed economies also play a role in elevating inflation. The institutions by which the trend of *wage rates* is set in the United States—particularly the leapfrogging of sequential three-year wage settlements reached in the course of tough and prolonged struggles over shares—can be an inflation machine. (This particular machine has been partially dismantled during the period of intense pressure on American manufacturing industries from the flood of imports. There has been no "leapfrogging" of settlements; cost-of-living wage adjustments have been removed, or modified.) The deterioration of *educational standards* at lower- and middle-school levels elevates the unemployment threshold below which inflation will accelerate; a massive general and technological educational effort will be essential to reach satisfactory employment levels, at satisfactory rates of inflation. Further extension of *protectionism* in the United States would contribute in an important way to domestic inflation; a gradual and orderly adjustment of the dollar toward a trade-determined valuation, together with intense effort to improve efficiency through direct investment, would in the end be much less inflationary, and has many other obvious advantages over protectionism. *All* forms of *indexation*—indexation of benefits in the transfer programs, indexation of wages, even indexation of tax brackets in the personal income tax code—are pro-inflationary, in that they compromise natural market forces that resist inflation, and remove the need to confront inflation consequences directly. (In effect, they restore the issue to the Federal Reserve, which must provide the funds to finance a rise in costs and incomes.) By transmuting transient elevations of cost into permanent income flows, indexation converts cyclical or sporadic price change into general inflation.

In the end, the inflation issue in the United States will be viewed in this broadly historical, institutional context, not simply as a battleground of conflicting theories. Modern inflation is a complex social phenomenon. Broad recognition of its real roots is necessary if inflation is to be managed effectively.

And in the end, we must hope that Congress and the Federal Reserve will develop programs for inflation control that will avert the violent assaults on the performance of the economic system as a whole that have characterized the last two decades. It is certainly not clear that we are there yet, however. The prudent observer will still have to watch the price indexes, and will still have to expect that a rise in the measured inflation rate will evoke the characteristic tightening of monetary conditions, and the characteristic rise in interest rates, that remain the conventional responses to inflation fears. And for the foreseeable future, he will have to watch the course of the dollar; significant weakness in the currency will continue to suggest some degree of imported inflation, as costs of imported materials and products rise. Indeed, the dollar, the price indexes, and interest rates, taken together, comprise the central challenge to the Federal Reserve, in its pursuit of policies that will foster growth and price stability in the new internationalized markets of the 1980s.

8
Epilogue: The Limitations of Numbers in a Mixed Economy

The awesome outpouring of numbers describing U.S. economic conditions is a stream of evidence. It bears on behavior, not on the structure of the system or, more philosophically, its nature. Nor do the figures say anything—directly, at least—about developing *changes* in the nature of the system. The flow of evidence on the direction of economic activity, and the tendency of economists to seek guides to the future from developments in comparable periods of the past, often suffer from a lack of awareness that the U.S. economy is a living, evolving structure, with laws of motion that derive mainly from forces much broader than can be captured in ordinary economic data. Understanding the future, it might be said, is too important to be left just to economists. Long statistical series, often running back decades, are really the tracks of an evolving animal; the relevance of the early segments of such data to the present and the future deteriorates with time. No review and study of the statistical stream is thus really complete, or really in proper perspective, absent an awareness of the forces that drive the structure of the economy, and what they portend for the future.

The bulk of economics operates on a paradigm of pure, free markets, in which purely self-interested individuals endlessly pursue their own advantage, under conditions of scarcity that pit one individual against another. If the world were really like this, then the gorgeous edifice of economic theory that is taught in graduate schools—and endlessly elaborated in the professional journals—would provide as good a description of economic events as physics provides for physical events, and economic predictions would be as valid as the predictions of physical scientists. It ain't necessarily so, of course; in fact, it necessarily ain't so.

There are individual markets in economics that are very close to perfectly free. Even for these markets, however, the predictive record leaves a great deal to be desired. At any point in time, superbly trained specialists even in pure markets will hold very different opinions about the future.

The scientific base of economics thus does not work very well even where the conditions are most conducive to its success. Beyond such narrow markets, however, looking at large aggregative chunks of the system or at the system as a whole, the paradigm of the free market fits the real world only very loosely. The real world is no longer composed solely of free markets freely interacting with each other. The United States, and indeed all major Western economies, contain large and growing nonmarket structures deliberately implanted in the system to achieve objectives that a free market will not reach, or will not reach within a desired time span. Their presence in the system reflects goals, objectives, priorities that arise out of essentially political and ethical rather than economic considerations.

Such a structure—a mixture of economic, political, social, cultural, and ethical structures—is called a **mixed economy.** The description of such a system and its probable future course simply cannot be found in economic theory alone; large parts of it lie in the huge body of legislation mandating certain kinds of activity, and in the federal revenue legislation providing the funds, as well as in the scores of government agencies regulating the limits of competitive behavior across broad sectors of the system.

The size and significance of these intrusions into the classical free market of economics are matters of heated political debate. The extreme positions range from warnings that increasing "socialization" is strangling the marketplace, and even threatening personal liberty, on the one hand, to the argument that they are hopelessly inadequate to protect ordinary citizens from exploitation by the market, and unable to protect them against the savaging of the environment by uncontrolled exploitation of technology. Not much can be learned from such heated political debate, but it is important, in appraising any longer-term future of the economy, to understand the real and durable roots of intervention.

An obvious first source and inspiration for intervention by public authorities into the marketplace is the political power conferred on an issue-oriented component of the electorate by a democratic political system. Labor, business, farmers, exporters, importers, the elderly, builders, even the ordinary individual struggling with the cost of living—all constitute constituencies that can bring their voting power to bear on a Congress and an administration. The much maligned bureaucracies that operate government become themselves a constituency for the development or continuation of interventions, in partial disregard of the public consequences. Selective groups of taxpayers that may cut across all other constituencies can be organized to support or oppose proposed alterations in the tax code. (Provisions called *tax expenditures*—losses of government revenue attributable to specific exemptions from general tax provisions—have recently run at an annual rate of $400 billion, more than twice the prevailing level of the budget deficit; they have been reduced somewhat by the tax reform effective in 1987.) Home builders and home buyers often unite to seek greater accommodation in housing finance; management and labor in individual industries unite to pursue protection against imports.

This source, which might be called parochial intervention in the service of individual self-interest, doubtless accounts for much of the aggregate intrusion into the marketplace. It is a big mistake, however, to assume that this is all there is to the imperfections of our markets—a mistake, because it suggests that the degree of intervention can be substantially reduced by a determined Congress and a determined administration. Some of the most important interventions carry the general support of the electorate as a whole, and conform to sensible economic prescriptions; others reflect deeply rooted ethical positions. The budget deficits of recent years—incurred by a Republican Administration in total defiance of its own orthodoxy—testify to the deep sociological and ethical supports of large federal programs.

Most of the wave of interventions that came in the wake of the desperate depression years of the 1930s are now generally accepted and beyond contention. They were intended to help stabilize an economic system, to forestall the destruction wrought by deep and prolonged recession. The regulation of securities markets; the insurance provided by the Federal Deposit Insurance Corporation and the Home Loan Bank Board; the centralization of credit control in the hands of a national central bank; the progressive personal income tax; the antitrust laws; the supervision provided by the Food and Drug Administration, the Federal Trade Commission, the Civil Aeronautics Board, and more recently the Environmental Protection Agency—to list only a few of the better known agencies—are in dispute only with respect to detail, not with respect to function. The grants of power to such agencies represent a broad public interest in reducing the instability the public learned to associate with the free market in the experience of the 1930s, and to provide a protection against the impacts of rapid technological development on the environment shared by all. Chapter 1 described the gradual accommodation of the American economy to the presence of these programs in the past four decades; it is an exercise of ideological fantasy to expect that such programs will lapse, or be substantially constrained.

Some of the costliest intrusions, in terms of government outlay, go beyond practical considerations to ethical justifications—efforts to achieve a fair, just, or compassionate society—to avoid extremes in the distribution of economic and noneconomic goods. These interventions reflect what might be called social compacts. They include social security, in which the young contribute to the support of the old; medical care, in which the healthy help to support the sick; unemployment compensation, in which the employed help to support the unemployed; the progressive income tax, in which the rich carry some of the burdens of the poor. The programs that carry the costs of these social compacts are very large, very expensive; in terms of burdens on the system, they far outweigh all the other intrusions. They account for the fact that the transfer payments flowing through the federal government, which now represent far and away the largest component of total federal outlay, enormously enhance the cost of government. They also reduce the raw economic incentives to work and to save. They carry a very nearly unqualified mandate, however; and expectations that their cost can be easily contained, let alone reduced, are not well founded. We had better plan on the existing level of social cost continuing into the future.

On the other hand, there is a lot of evidence, in Europe as well as in the United States, that the growth of interventions is abating and their rate of increase subsiding to a more settled, more manageable, and less inflationary rate.

A considerable portion of the energy entering into ethical interventions in the system has doubtless been used up in the institutional transformation of the past forty years, particularly the accelerated rate of change from the mid-1960s to the end of the 1970s. The rhetoric of the attack on the free market and its cruelties has been blunted by the obvious growth of non-market distributive and social efforts. The further pursuit of distributive goals seems to have carried a rising marginal cost in the inflation of the 1970s, and perhaps also a rising public irritation with the costs.

It is far more widely recognized today than it was ten years ago that much of any incremental interventions will find their effects dissipated by renewed inflation, and that there is no truly effective way of controlling inflation other than simply slowing the rate at which we do inflationary things. In the great trade-off between ethically justified interventions into the market, and the market institutions themselves, there is no free lunch; indeed, the price of the lunch obviously rose sharply during the 1970s. The self-interest that is the source of energy in the free market is still a principal motivation to efficient activity; this useful, dependable, and candid if not inspiring motivation is bound to be compromised in some degree by further elevations of intervention. The experience of the business recovery in late 1982, running into mid-1984, revealed large opportunities to improve the well-being of all by preserving efficiency, incentives, investment, and growth. If there has been a "Reagan revolution," its source may lie in its successful marshaling of resistance to further growth of social programs.

The mixed economy thus seems to have reached a condition of general maturity in the United States and in most other developed economies. The developed structure of nonmarket activities is unlikely to be curtailed; and the funds for financing them therefore, in the end, must be found. Neither, however, are they likely to enter a new round of proliferation and rising cost. The experience of the U.S. economy in the 1980s results from a much tougher international economic environment than has prevailed at any time since the end of World War II. The United States no longer owns the world economy; it must find its competitive place in a world economy of tough competitors; its efficiency—its "competitiveness"—is now a crucial dimension of its world economic performance, and therefore of the standard of living it can support at home. International competition—with such competent competitors as Japan, Germany and other European nations, and a host of newly industrializing nations whose costs are violently competitive with our own—constrain our options; we must control our appetite even for the "social goals" provided by government. To the extent that we fail to live within our means, this new competitive world will impose restraints upon us, through deterioration of our currency, higher inflation, and higher interest rates.

This appraisal of the institutional condition of the system suggests a number of observations about the future of the U.S. economy:

First, the social costs in the system will not go away, but they appear to have stabilized as a percentage of total activity. The inflationary thrust induced by the growth of these programs has subsided, but a residual and potential inflation still exists in their underfinancing. The closure (not necessarily total, but substantial) of the ongoing budget deficit would remove this latent inflation threat. At this writing, there is a consensus on the need to control the federal deficit, but consensus on the policies—the specific constraints on spending, the specific enhancements of revenue—is still to take shape.

The maturing of the structure of the mixed economy—the end of the relative surge of costs—enlarges the opportunity for stable and vigorous growth of the economy as a whole in the future. Among the functions of the great social compacts incorporated in the mixed economy was the loosening of the link between income and production (lower production means lower income means lower demand means lower production, and so on, as described in chapter 4) that is an inherent instability in a free-market economy. Although the programs carry heavy cost, they mark an increase in stability—a lessening of the energy of the business cycle—that is part of the reward for the costs.

The mixed economy is not a beautiful structure; it defies and irritates theoretical purists of all persuasions. Complex, changing, nontheoretical, it is the real world in which we live, the world reflected in the diverse and often conflicting numbers that describe the oncoming future. It is a *living, changing* reality that has evolved as a continuing resolution of the pressures between a democratic political system and a market-oriented economy. As with all the products of an evolutionary process, it seems well adapted to the political, ethical, sociological, and technological pressures that have shaped it. It will doubtless continue to evolve in the future. Making good judgments about the future will continue to require not just numerical evidence, but also broad appraisal of the society of which the economy is a part. And in the thoroughly internationalized world that has emerged in the 1980s—internationalized for consumer markets, for capital goods markets, for financial flows—it will be necessary continuously to appraise the behavior of the world economic structure that surrounds and constrains U.S. economic experience.

At this writing, it is far too early to appraise the ultimate consequences of the stock market crash of late 1987. But the world that built the inflated and vulnerable financial markets of the 1980s is a world of mixed economies, featuring large governments with large powers and large responsibilities. This is a great—perhaps a controlling—difference between the late 1920s and the late 1980s. The degree to which pragmatic, cooperative use is made of the power of mixed economies to respond to dangerous developments will play a large role in determining outcomes, at home and among our trading partners.

Appendix A
Alphabetical List of Series

Assets and liabilities outstanding, Federal Reserve, p. 87
Average hourly and weekly earnings, U.S. Department of Labor, p. 83

Balance of payments, U.S. Department of Commerce, p. 129
Borrowed reserves, Federal Reserve, p. 117
Business cycle, National Bureau of Economic Research, p. 89
Business gross income, U.S. Department of Commerce, p. 51

Capacity utilization rate, Federal Reserve, p. 74
Capital consumption adjustment, U.S. Department of Commerce, p. 42
Capital consumption allowances, U.S. Department of Commerce, p. 20
Capital markets, Federal Reserve, p. 88
Capital outlay by business, U.S. Department of Commerce, p. 72
Change in business inventories, U.S. Department of Commerce, p. 33
Commodity price index, Commodity Research Bureau, Inc., p. 83
Consumer attitudes, University of Michigan, p. 68
Consumer credit, Federal Reserve, p. 68
Consumer price index, U.S. Department of Labor, p. 81
Corporate profits, U.S. Department of Commerce, p. 42
Cyclical deficits, U.S. Department of Commerce, p. 111
Cyclically adjusted deficits, U.S. Department of Commerce, p. 112

Debt outstanding, Federal Reserve, p. 87
Demand for credit, Federal Reserve, p. 124
Depreciation allowance, U.S. Department of Commerce, p. 51
Diffusion index, The Conference Board, p. 100
Discount rate, Federal Reserve, p. 117
Disposable personal income, U.S. Department of Commerce, p. 46

Employment and unemployment, U.S. Department of Labor, p. 78

Personal consumption expenditures, U.S. Department of Commerce, p. 28
Personal income, U.S. Department of Commerce, p. 40
Personal saving, U.S. Department of Commerce, p. 47
Plant and equipment spending, U.S. Department of Commerce, p. 101
Producer price index, U.S. Department of Labor, p. 81
Producers' durable equipment, U.S. Department of Commerce, p. 33
Productivity, U.S. Department of Labor, p. 84
Property income, U.S. Department of Commerce, p. 46

Real GNP, U.S. Department of Commerce, p. 25
Residential construction, U.S. Department of Commerce, p. 32
Retail sales, U.S. Department of Commerce, p. 68

Saving and investment, U.S. Department of Commerce, p. 55
Statistical discrepancy, U.S. Department of Commerce, p. 39

Total manufacturing and trade, U.S. Department of Commerce, p. 77
Transfer payments, U.S. Department of Commerce, p. 37

Unincorporated business, U.S. Department of Commerce, p. 50
Unit labor costs, U.S. Department of Labor, p. 84

Work week, U.S. Department of Labor, p. 80

Value of securities, Standard & Poor's, Inc., p. 104

For additional information about series listed in this appendix, please contact the following agencies:

Commodity Research Bureau
75 Montgomery Street
Jersey City, New Jersey 07302
Telephone: (201) 451-7500

The Conference Board
845 Third Avenue
New York, New York 10022
Telephone: (212) 759-0900

Department of the Treasury
3021 GAO Building
Washington, D.C. 20226
Telephone: (202) 566-2000

Federal Reserve Board
Publications Systems, MP-510
Washington, D.C. 20551
Telephone: (202) 452-3000

National Bureau of Economic Research
1050 Massachusetts Avenue
Cambridge, Massachusetts 02138
Telephone: (617) 868-3905

Office of Management and Budget
Old Executive Office Building, NW
Washington, D.C. 20503
Telephone: (202) 395-3000

Standard & Poor's Corporation, Inc.
25 Broadway
New York, New York 10004
Telephone: (212) 208-1199

University of Michigan
Institute of Social Research
P.O. Box 1248
Ann Arbor, Michigan 48106-1248
Telephone: (313) 763-5224

U.S. Department of Commerce
Bureau of Economic Analysis (BEA)
1401 "K" Street, NW
Washington, D.C. 20230
Telephone: (202) 377–2000

U.S. Department of Labor
441 "G" Street, NW
Washington, D.C. 20212
Telephone: (202) 655-4000

Appendix B:
Approximate Release Dates for Monthly Statistics*

MONDAY	TUESDAY	WEDNESDAY	THURSDAY	FRIDAY
			1 • Construction Expenditures▲ • Manufacturers' Shipments, Inventories, Orders▲ • Interest Rates	**2** • Employment Situation • Help-Wanted Index▲
5 • Auto Sales • Commodity Indexes	**6**	**7** • Consumer Credit▲	**8**	**9** • Wholesale Trade▲
12	**13** • Housing Completions▲	**14** • Merchandise Trade▲ • Advance Retail Sales • Auto Sales	**15** • Manufacturing and Trade Inventories and Sales▲	**16** • Producer Price Index • Industrial Production Index
19 • Capacity Utilization	**20** • Housing Starts • Building Permits	**21**	**22** • Treasury Statement	**23** • Advance Durables Goods Orders • Consumer Price Index • Real Earnings
26 • Auto Sales • Personal Income	**27** • Construction Contract Awards	**28**	**29**	**30** • Housing Sales • Agricultural Sales • Composite Index • Machine Tool Shipments and New Orders

* For prior month, unless otherwise indicated
▲ For two months prior

Appendix C:
Approximate Release Dates for Quarterly Statistics*

MONDAY	TUESDAY	WEDNESDAY	THURSDAY	FRIDAY
			1	**2**
5	**6**	**7**	**8**	**9**
12 • Capital Appropriations	**13**	**14**	**15** • Quarterly Financial Report-Manufacturing	**16**
19 • U.S. International Transactions	**20** • Plant and Equipment▲	**21**	**22**	**23** • GNP • Personal Income • Corporate Profits
26 • Collective Bargaining Settlements • Flow of Funds▲▲	**27** • Employment Cost Index	**28** • Housing Vacancies	**29** • U.S. Import and Export Price Indexes • Productivity and Costs	**30**

✱ For prior quarter, unless otherwise indicated
▲ For current quarter
▲▲ For two quarters prior

About the Authors

Albert T. Sommers is among the most widely respected economists serving the U.S. business community. In his thirty-seven years at The Conference Board, thirteen of them as its chief economist, he has advised literally hundreds of companies on economic conditions and the future course of the U.S. economy.

Mr. Sommers is currently senior fellow and economic counsellor to The Conference Board. He is economic adviser to The Ford Foundation, The American Express Company, Bankers Trust Company, and Drexel Burnham Lambert, among others. He is a director of several industrial and financial institutions and of the National Bureau of Economic Research, a Fellow of the National Association of Business Economists, and a former member of the Columbia University economics faculty. He is editor and publisher of "The Sommers Letter," a continuing appraisal of the national and international economic outlook read by more than 2,500 business executives and government officials here and abroad.

Lucie R. Blau, an economist and assistant to the senior fellow at The Conference Board, has collaborated with Mr. Sommers on a host of publications extending over 25 years, and is an assistant editor of "The Sommers Letter."

About the Conference Board

The Conference Board is a business information service whose purpose is to assist senior executives and other leaders in arriving at sound decisions. Since its founding in 1916, The Board has been creating close personal networks of leaders who exchange experience and judgment on significant issues in management practice, economics, and public policy. The networks are supported by an international program of research and meetings which The Conference Board staff of more than 350 persons carries out from offices in New York, Ottawa, and Brussels.

More than 3,200 organizations in over 50 nations participate in The Conference Board's work as Associates. The Board is a not-for-profit corporation and the greatest share of its financial support comes from business concerns, many with worldwide operations. The Board also has many Associates among labor unions, colleges and universities, government agencies, libraries, and trade and professional associations.